ULTIMATE
BRAIN-BOOSTING
TOOLKIT

Dr Shireen Stephen holds a Ph.D. in Health Psychology and an M.Phil. and M.Sc. in Applied Psychology. She is a counselling psychologist, researcher, writer and editor. She is well known for her episodic memory of remembering dates and connected events. She is also renowned for her auditory memory of remembering clients and their counselling sessions—even years later—without taking down any notes!

She has also authored *Smart Guide for Awesome Memory*, *The 4-Week Memory Challenge* and *Train Your Brain: Ultimate Memory Hacks*.

THE
ULTIMATE
BRAIN-BOOSTING
TOOLKIT

Shireen Stephen

RUPA

Published by
Rupa Publications India Pvt. Ltd 2019
7/16, Ansari Road, Daryaganj
New Delhi 110002

Illustrations by Ritabrata Joardar

P-ISBN: 978-93-5333-399-7
E-ISBN: 978-93-5333-400-0

Fifth impression 2024

10 9 8 7 6 5

This book is dedicated with love to all the super-intelligent influencers in my life: my husband—Mr Rabin Stephen— my parents—Mr Reginald Solomon and Professor Shantha Solomon—my father-in-law and late mother-in-law—Professor T. Sargunam Stephen and Professor Jane Mangalam Stephen—and my late grandfather—Dr L.B.M. Joseph.

Contents

Chapter 1

Introduction

What has four feet at dawn,
two at midday and three at twilight?

One of the earliest and oldest puzzles known to the Western world is the Riddle of the Sphynx (1800–1600 BCE). In Greek mythology, the Sphynx is a monster with the head and bust of a woman, the body of a lion and the wings of a bird. Legend has it that she would sit at the entrance of Thebes and ask travellers entering the city the riddle mentioned above. If they answered it incorrectly, they would be killed immediately. However, if they answered correctly, she vowed to destroy herself. It is said that the only person to solve this riddle was Oedipus, who answered, 'A human being, who crawls on all fours as a baby (dawn of life), walks on two feet as an adult (midday of life) and with a walking stick in old age (twilight of life).' He was later made the king of Thebes for destroying the Sphynx.

Another story associated with a puzzle that hails from ancient Greece is that of the Greek mathematician Archimedes (287–212 BCE), who was tasked to find out if the crown of King Hiero II was made of pure gold or if there was some impurity, such as silver, mixed with it. He was to do this without damaging the crown in any way. This meant that he could not melt it or test portions of it—it had to remain intact. Archimedes mulled over this problem for a long time but could not find a solution. One day, while taking a bath, he observed that the water in the bathtub rose when he got in. He suddenly realized that he could use the same principle to determine the density of the crown. By dividing the mass of the crown by the volume of water it displaced, he found that the density of the crown was much lower than the density of solid gold. Silver had indeed been mixed in it and the crown was not 'pure' gold.

Human beings have always been fascinated with puzzles and brain-teasers. Archimedes himself was probably the first person in history to build a puzzle. It was known as the Loculus Archimedis, or Archemedes' Box, and was a cross between a jigsaw puzzle and a tangram. Historical records reveal that he enjoyed coming up with challenging problems for his peers to solve. Biblical kings such as Solomon and Hiram used to hold riddle contests. More recently, famous writers such as Edgar Allan Poe, Lewis Carroll and J.R.R. Tolkien, entrepreneurs such as Leonardo da Vinci and Benjamin Franklin, and architects such as Ernő Rubik have all been fascinated with developing and solving puzzles. This fascination continues today in the form of brain-teasers in newspapers, quiz shows on television, game tournaments and, of course, puzzle books.

Some puzzles were developed as tools for learning while others were developed just for fun. For example, the Rubik's Cube was originally designed to teach students of architecture to think in three dimensions, while the crossword was the brainchild of Arthur Wynne, who designed it for the newspaper *New York World* in 1913 just to entertain his readers.

This book brings you puzzles that teach and train certain aspects of cognition (thought) and memory while making them entertaining and fun as well.

Benefits of Puzzles

Puzzles and brain-teasers have several benefits. The first major benefit is that solving puzzles keeps your brain fit and strong. In children and adolescents, it can hone cognitive (thinking) abilities and can keep the brain sharp and agile. In adults, solving puzzles can help them solve everyday problems logically without much stress and also improve focus and concentration. In older adults, working on puzzles on a daily basis can keep their brains active and may also help stave off or slow down the onset of brain degenerative diseases such as Parkinson's and Alzheimer's.

The second major benefit of solving puzzles on a daily basis is that it can be applied to real-world problems as well. For example, just as you would solve a mathematical puzzle by using hard logic, you may be able to apply the same logic in a stressful situation either with your boss at work, a fast-approaching examination that you have not prepared for yet or with a classmate who is bullying you. In the same way, once you get accustomed to using an out-of-the-box approach to solve riddles, you can apply the same mode of creative thinking to tackle everyday issues. This not only makes life less stressful but also makes problem-solving more enjoyable!

The third major advantage is that it activates cognitive abilities that you might not use on a daily basis. This in turn activates different parts of your brain that help in improving memory, aptitude for problem-solving, focus and attention, reasoning skills, understanding and grasping ability, creativity and reaction time to any problem that may come your way.

Puzzles also develop the three elements of intelligence: creativity, logic and analytical skills. They are a great means of conquering boredom, depression, anxiety and stress, and can lead to personal discovery, motivation, self-control and satisfaction. Just as you need to keep your body fit and healthy, you also need to keep your mind active to improve the health of your brain. Solving puzzles, brain-teasers and riddles for at least half an hour every day is all it takes to succeed in keeping your mind healthy and fit! A scientific study by Sherry Willis, Sharon Tennstedt and Michael Marsiske[1] at the University of Florida discovered that solving puzzles staves off mental decline, bolsters the brain and sharpens logical skills in adults in the same way that physical exercise protects and strengthens the body. The study suggested that people needed to start with easy puzzles and graduate to more difficult ones to reap the full benefits of brain training. These results have been supported by many other scientific studies.

Cognitive Functions

Take a moment to observe all the thoughts running through your mind at this very moment. Are they swirling around in your mind? Or are they cascading down one after the other in quick succession? Is there a song or a tune that has been playing endlessly in your mind? You will notice that your brain is always active. It is constantly perceiving, processing, planning, organizing and remembering. Yet, you don't notice most of your brain's activity as you move through your daily routine. This is only one facet of the complex processes involved in cognition. Simply put, cognition is thinking, and it encompasses the processes associated with perception, knowledge, problem-solving, judgement, language and memory.

As you can see, your brain has various cognitive functions. You may be more proficient in one area but need some practice

---

[1]Sherry L. Willis, Sharon L. Tennstedt, Michael Mirsarke, 'Long-term Effects of Cognitive Training on Everyday Functional Outcomes in Older Adults', *Journal of American Medical Association* 296(23):2805-2814. 2006.

in another. For example, you may be good at solving logical problems but may not be as good with creative problems. Or you may have great linguistic skills but may not be as good at solving mathematical problems. Since different parts of your brain are responsible for specific cognitive functions, it is imperative to train these areas of your brain to boost its overall performance. This can be done by solving puzzles and brain games that are specially designed to boost specific areas of your brain.

The puzzles and brain games in this book test and train ten aspects of cognitive functions listed below. These will be discussed in more detail at the beginning of each chapter.

1. **Logical thinking** helps you think in a disciplined way, basing your thoughts on fact and evidence.
2. **Analytical thinking** helps hone your powers of deduction, problem-solving and reasoning.
3. **Verbal reasoning** trains your language and comprehension, vocabulary, reading, etc.
4. **Imagination and creativity** helps hone your imagination, creativity and resourcefulness by inventing new concepts and ideas.
5. **Numerical reasoning** hones your numerical aptitude, problem-solving, and helps in deciphering codes, abstract symbols and formulae.
6. **Lateral thinking** helps you think creatively and find out-of-the-box solutions to problems.
7. **Active observation** helps hone your visual, acoustic, olfactory, gustatory and kinaesthetic senses and provides you with an eye for detail.
8. **Spatial memory** helps improve visualization as well as the ability to transform and manipulate spatial figures mentally.
9. **Processing speed** helps you process information quickly

by scanning, discriminating and sequencing simple visual information.

10. **Working memory** trains your short-term memory and your ability to actively maintain information in conscious awareness, perform some operation or manipulation with it and produce a result.

How to Use This Book

This book is chock-full of games, secret codes, brain-teasers, puzzles, riddles and many more fun activities, all designed to boost the power of your brain to make it fit and active. It consists of ten chapters that test and train a particular cognitive function. Each chapter consists of five exercises with increasing levels of difficulty starting at the beginner's level and moving on to the expert level. The difficulty levels are indicated in each exercise as follows:

*Easy
**Intermediate
***Advanced
****Expert

Each exercise takes about 10–20 minutes to solve. Try and complete at least one exercise per day. You can either choose to move from one chapter to the next, working through the puzzles and exercises in a systematic way by training one cognitive function at a time; or you can choose to do one exercise from each chapter, which will train different cognitive functions simultaneously. However, it is recommended that you start with the beginner-level exercises and work your way through the tougher levels.

Some exercises that may seem simple to you may be considered difficult by others. Do not be daunted by the tougher exercises—you will reap the benefits of brain training only when you challenge your brain. Attempt all exercises in each chapter. If you are unclear about how a particular puzzle works or are stumped, take a quick peek at part of the answer and then try and work out the rest of the puzzle by yourself. Resist the temptation to turn straight to the answers when you tackle a puzzle. All answers are within your grasp—they just need a bit of thought! Answers are provided at the end of the book.

Try not to attempt too many exercises at once, as this can tire your brain and slow you down, leaving room for possible mistakes. If you wish to solve more than one exercise at a time, take a break of about ten minutes and use this time to do something completely different (something that does not require a lot of mental work) before getting back to the exercises. Most exercises require you to write or draw something, so keep a pencil and a few extra sheets of paper handy. Some exercises might have a time limit, so having a stopwatch handy may also help.

While this book contains about 450 puzzles and exercises that will keep you busy for a few weeks or months, brain training is a lifelong activity. Make it a point to solve puzzles in daily newspapers, magazines and online on a regular basis. If a certain type of puzzle interests you, try finding it online. However, make sure you keep challenging yourself by working out increasingly difficult puzzles.

This book is designed for children and adults alike and is more appropriate for ages 12 and above. The whole premise of boosting your brainpower is to have fun while challenging your brain. So sit back, relax and enjoy yourself!

Chapter 2

Just Deduce It!

Logical thinking keeps you from wasting time worrying or
hoping. It prevents disappointment.
—JODI PICOULT

When we say that something is logical, what we mean is that it makes sense. Logical thinking is the process in which one uses reasoning and cold, hard facts consistently to come to a conclusion. It may also involve combining a set of premises to reach a logical conclusion. For example, if A = B and B = C, then logically, C = A. Enhancing logical reasoning is learning to pay closer attention to details. Logic requires no prior knowledge, no mathematical or linguistic skills—just the ability to use reason. Honing this skill improves your powers of observation and deduction.

The following puzzles may seem tricky but if you follow the reasoning that eliminates the impossible choices until only the correct solution remains, you will acquire the mastery needed to tackle any problem of logical deduction.

Exercise 1: Relative Relationships*

1. Ann runs faster than Nikki
    Nikki runs faster than Jemma.
    Ann runs faster than Jemma.

If the first two statements are true, then the third statement is:

True   False   Uncertain

2. Mr Smith has four daughters. Each of his daughters has a brother. How many children does Mr Smith have?

3. Which statement is false?
   a) Statement D is true.
   b) Statement A is false.
   c) Statement B is false.
   d) Statement C is true.

4. Jane and Jemima are called Stephen and Jones, but it is unclear if it is Jane Stephen and Jemima Jones or Jane Jones and Jemima Stephen. Given that two of the following statements are false, what is Jane's surname?
   a) Jane's surname is Jones.
   b) Jane's surname is Stephen.
   c) Jemima's surname is Stephen.

5. Using the following clues, place the letters between A and I in the grid below. 'Above/below' refers to two letters in the same column. 'Left/right' refers to two letters in the same row.
   a) C is below G and above E
   b) D is above A and to the right of F
   c) F is above I and to the left of D
   d) A is above H and to the right of I
   e) H is to the right of B and to the left of E

6. There is only one correct answer among the following answers. Which is it?
    a) Answer A
    b) Answer A and B
    c) Answer B and C

7. Paul is taller than Jerry
    Bob is shorter than Paul

    Which of the following statements do you know for certain?
    a) Jerry is taller than Bob
    b) Bob is taller than Jerry
    c) It cannot be determined if Bob or Jerry is taller

8. Four friends are sharing a pizza. They decide that the oldest friend will get the extra piece. Radha is two months older than Georgie, who is three months younger than Priya. Kelly is one month older than Georgie. Who should get the extra piece of pizza?
    a) Radha
    b) Georgie
    c) Priya
    d) Kelly

9. Four people are painting Mr Cree's house. Sam is painting the front of the house. Ronny is in the alley behind the house, painting the back. Joseph is painting the window frames on the northern side, Kiran is on the south. If Sam switches places with Joseph, and Joseph then switches places with Kiran, where is Kiran?
   a) In the alley behind the house
   b) On the north side of the house
   c) On the south side of the house
   d) In front of the house

10. Last night, Priya and her husband invited their friends (two couples) to dinner. The six of them sat at a round table.

    Next day, Priya describes the seating arrangement as:

    - George sat on the left of the woman who sat on the left of the man who sat on the left of Asha.
    - Preethi sat on the left of the man who sat on the left of the woman who sat on the left of the man who sat on the left of the woman who sat on the left of my husband.
    - Pradeep sat on the left of the woman who sat on the left of Dilip.
    - I did not sit beside my husband.

    Where is each person sitting? What is the name of Priya's husband?

    Hint: It may help if you draw the round table and place each person on their seat.

Exercise 2: Disconnect Four*

1. Draw either X or O in every empty space in the following grid, taking care not to have any lines of four or more Xs or Os either horizontally, vertically or diagonally.

X				O	O		O
	O		X				X
		O	O		X		X
O	X	O		O			O
O						X	
	X		X		X	X	X
		X		O			X
X			O	O			O

2. The following puzzle is slightly different from the one above. Fill up all squares with Xs and Os. All rows and columns need to have four Xs and four Os; however, there must not be more than **two** of the same letter in direct succession. For example, a row with XXOOXOOXO is valid but a row with XXXOOXOO is invalid because of the three Xs. This rule is valid only horizontally and vertically but not diagonally (it's okay to have more than two Xs or Os diagonally).

X	X		X			O	
X	X	O				X	
			O				
				O	X		O
O		O	O				
				X			
	X				O	X	X
	O			X		X	X

3. Move all four blocks from the first rod to the third rod in the least number of moves. Only one block can be moved at a time. A bigger block cannot be placed over a smaller block. All blocks need to be arranged on the third rod in the same order as they are in the first rod.

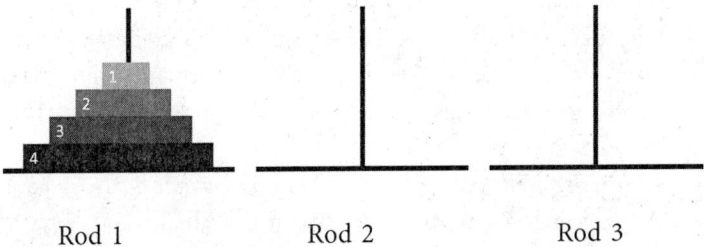

Rod 1   Rod 2   Rod 3

Exercise 3: Tricky Logic**

The answers to the following questions are not as straightforward as they seem. Read the questions carefully before answering.

1. A man wants to enter an exclusive club, but he doesn't know the password. Another man walks to the door and the doorman says 12. The man says 6, and is let in. Another man walks up and the doorman says 6. The man says 3, and is let in. Thinking he has heard enough, he walks up to the door and the doorman says 10. He says 5, and he isn't let in. What should he have said?

2. At the centre of a round lake lies a beautiful lotus. The lotus doubles in size every day. After exactly 20 days, the lotus covers the whole lake. How many days would it have taken the lotus to cover half the lake?

3. Two men were born at the same time. They both grew up, travelled the world and died at the same time. However, they did not live to the same age. How?

4. Paul and Martha are married and have two children, one of whom is a girl. Assuming that the probability of each gender is 1/2, what is the probability that the other child is also a girl?

5. An Arab sheikh tells his two sons to race their camels to a distant city to see who will inherit his fortune. The one whose camel is slower will win. After wandering aimlessly for days, the brothers ask a wise man for guidance. Upon receiving the advice, they jump on the camels and race to the city as fast as they can. What does the wise man say to them?

6. Three disciples wanted to find out who the wisest amongst them was, so they turned to their leader, asking him to resolve their dispute. Their leader told them that he would blindfold all of them and paint either a red or a blue dot on each man's forehead. 'When I take your

blindfolds off,' he said, 'if you see at least one red dot on another man's forehead, you must raise your hand. The one who guesses the colour of the dot on his own forehead first wins.'

The leader blindfolded his three disciples and painted red dots on all of them. When he took their blindfolds off, all three men raised their hands as the rules required, and sat in silence, pondering. Finally, one of them said, 'I have a red dot on my forehead.'

How did he know?

7. There are three switches on the ground floor. Each switch corresponds to one of the three light bulbs on the first floor, which you cannot see. You can turn the switches on and off or leave them in any position. How would you identify which switch corresponds to which light bulb, if you are only allowed one trip upstairs?

8. A family of two parents and two children (a son and a daughter) needs to cross a river that has no bridge. The only way to get to the other side is to ask a nearby fisherman if he can lend them his boat. However, the boat is very small and can either carry one adult or two children at a time. How does the family get to the other side and then return the boat to the fisherman?

9. If the following list is a list of ten words, logically, what would the first two words be?

————

————

Third
Fourth
Fifth
Sixth
Seventh

Eighth

Ninth

Tenth

10. What letter can you place on the line below to form a complete word?

S E Q U E N C _

Exercise 4: What Comes Next?**

Look at the sequences of boxes below and logically work out what figure should come next. Choose your answer from options A to E. Each question may require a different kind of logic in order to solve it.

1.

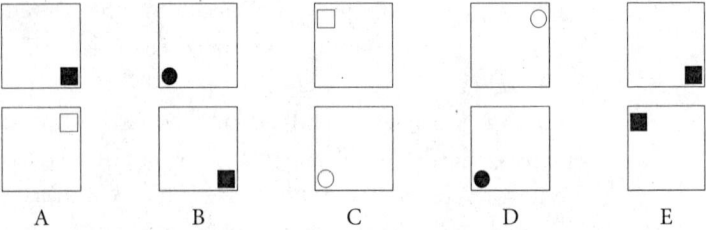

A   B   C   D   E

2.

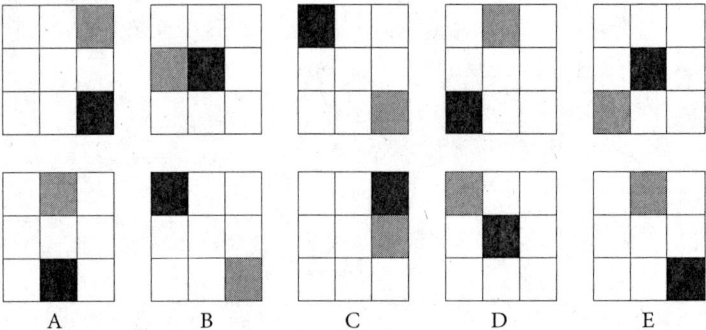

A   B   C   D   E

3.

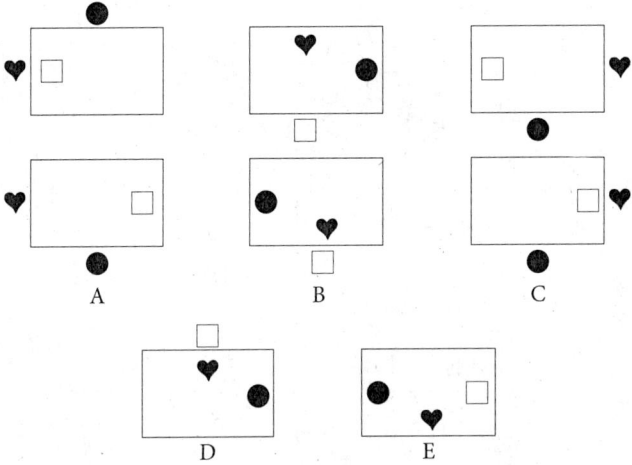

4.

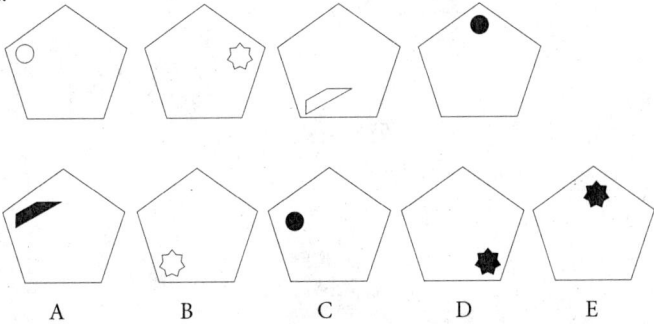

5.

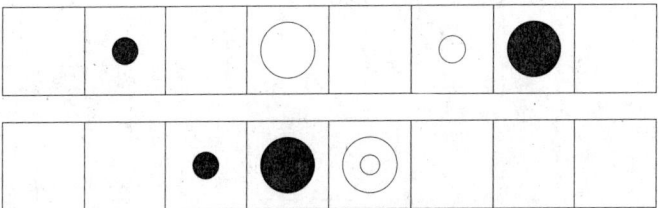

A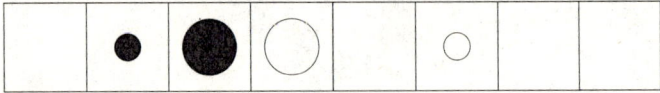

B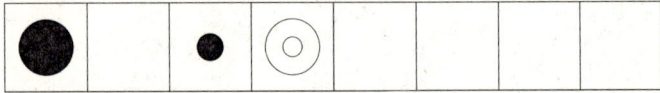

C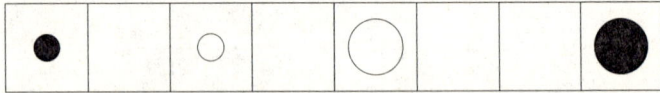

D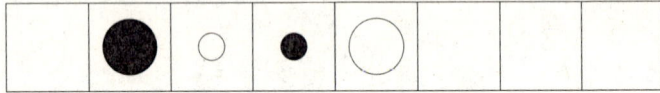

E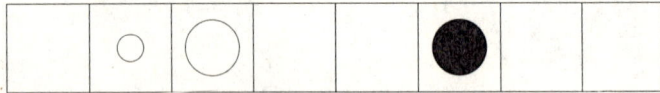

6.

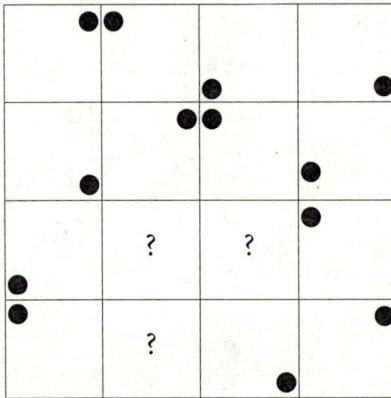

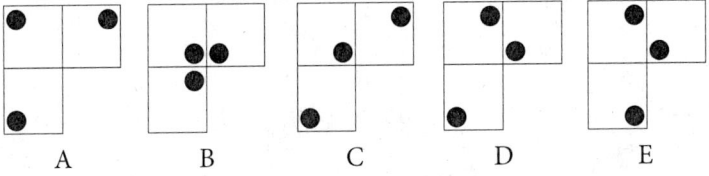

A   B   C   D   E

7.

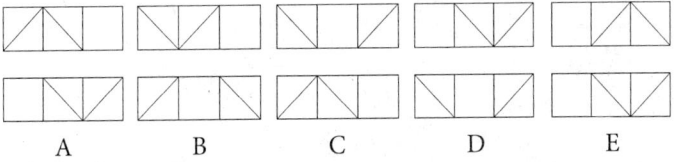

A   B   C   D   E

8.

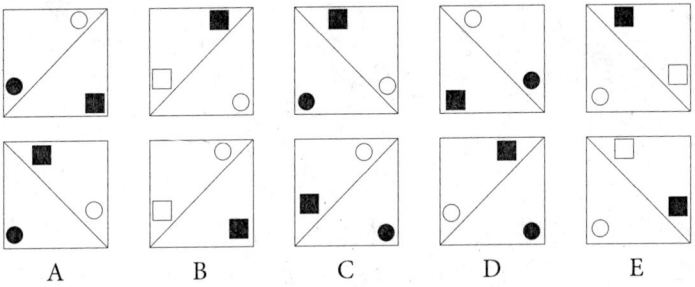

A   B   C   D   E

9.

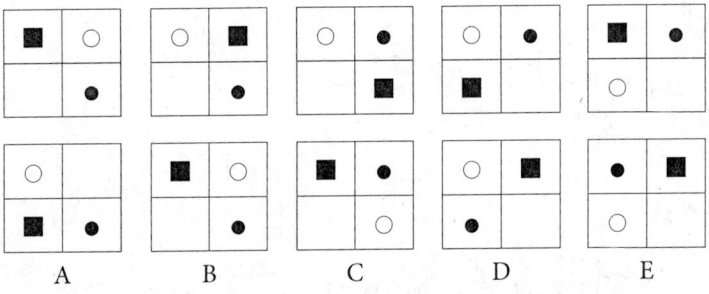

A   B   C   D   E

10.

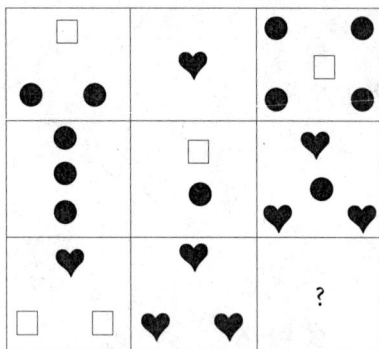

   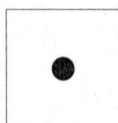 

| A | B | C | D | E |

Exercise 5: Analogically Speaking***

Analogies are tests of logical reasoning that assess your ability to find the logical relationships between words and their meanings. Look at the relationship between the first pair of words and then apply the same logic to the next pair of words.

1. Libra is to scales as Aries is to
    a) fish
    b) bull
    c) goat
    d) ram

2. Marathon is to race as hibernation is to
    a) winter
    b) bear

    c) dream

    d) sleep

3. Elated is to despondent as enlightened is to
    a) miserable
    b) aware
    c) tolerant
    d) ignorant

4. Exercise is to gym as eating is to
    a) diet
    b) fitness
    c) restaurant
    d) food

5. Candle is to lamp is to torch as hut is to cottage is to
    a) tent
    b) dwelling
    c) house
    d) light

6. Ant is to fly is to bee as hamster is to squirrel is to
    a) rodent
    b) mouse
    c) wasp
    d) pig

7. Tadpole is to frog is to amphibian as lamb is to sheep is to
    a) animal
    b) wool
    c) farm
    d) mammal

8. Frame is to picture as

    a) criminal is to gang
    b) binding is to book
    c) carpenter is to artist
    d) nail is to hammer

9. Bicycle is to tyre as
    a) puppy is to dog
    b) flower is to petal
    c) shoes is to sandals
    d) ball is to bat

10. Examine is to scrutinize as
    a) throb is to pulsate
    b) ballet is to dancer
    c) lose is to find
    d) walk is to run

WHAT MORE CAN YOU DO?

Logical Thinking

- Keep trying new activities that are different from each other but have just one solution. Crocheting, cross-stitching, knitting patterns and other forms of embroidery are just a few examples of these activities.
- Play games that require logic. Examples include chess, Chinese chequers, Mastermind, Monopoly, Prime Climb, etc.
- Take at least fifteen minutes to half an hour out of your day to solve logic puzzles such as sudoku, kakuro, Hanjie, futoshiki, Calcudoku, Hitori, Slitherlink, Skyscraper, Nurikabe, etc.
- Learn a musical instrument. While this may seem more like art, you require hard logic to follow timing, read music

and translate that music to specific finger movements on a keyboard, guitar, violin or another instrument.

- Read. Read anything, whether it is newspapers, magazines, fiction, non-fiction, fantasy fiction—it doesn't matter. Reading broadens your perspectives and your views on many subjects and this plays a role in your behaviour and attitudes.

- Look at everyday problems from a logical perspective and take a problem-solving approach while tackling them. Most problems in our daily lives can be solved logically and practically. When we allow ourselves to get emotional about problems, we take a longer time to deal with them, and this can lead to overwhelming stress. This stress can either be avoided or reduced substantially by dealing with the problem logically.

- Try to avoid making assumptions in daily situations; rather, stick to facts as much as possible.

Chapter 3

Analyse This!

The best magic always results from ecstasies of logic.
—ALBAN BERG

Analytical thinking involves thinking about things in a critical way before arriving at solution. People with strong analytical skills have the ability to investigate a problem methodically and arrive at a solution in a timely, efficient manner. They also have the ability to use clear, logical steps and make sound judgements based on hard facts before executing an action.

Analytical thinking might sound technical but we use these skills in everyday work when detecting patterns, brainstorming, observing and interpreting data, theorizing, planning, processing new information and making decisions based on multiple factors and options. These skills are essential for jobs in business analytics, architecture, marketing, project management, accounting, banking, business development, software programming, law, medicine, science, etc.

In this chapter, a problem will be presented to you with just a few clues that by themselves may not lead to the solution. You will need to analyse these clues by applying logic, which will then lead you to the solution. Analytical thinking helps you understand the cause and effect of certain phenomena and hones your deductive reasoning skills.

The following exercises may seem simple, but it is important to take time to read the question properly, pay attention to the details and see if you can crack them.

Exercise 1: Elementary, My Dear Watson*

You are provided with a few clues to the following mysteries. Put your detective cap on and see if you can deduce and solve all the mysteries.

1. A man was shot dead in his car. There were no powder marks on his clothing, which indicated that the murderer was outside the car. However, all the windows were up and all the doors were locked, with the key still in the ignition. How was he murdered?

2. An undercover detective infiltrated an oil-smuggling ring. However, just a day before he was going to bust the gang, he went missing. Before he disappeared, he had the presence of mind to leave a note for you: 710 57735 34, 5508 51 7718. You have four suspects: Bill, John, Todd and Luke. Can you break the detective's code and find out which of your four suspects is the culprit?

3. Luke was kidnapped and the kidnappers sent a ransom note to his family asking for one lakh rupees in unmarked notes. The money was to be put into a suitcase and kept under a bench in a nearby park. Luke's brother Thomas was to place the suitcase under the park bench at 8 o'clock sharp that night. However, while he was on his way to the bench, somebody hit him on the head from behind and ran away with the suitcase. When you questioned him, Thomas said, 'It was very dark in the park but I managed to see the attacker. He had red hair, was wearing a V-neck sweater and baggy blue jeans.' You immediately arrest Thomas on suspicion of kidnapping his own brother. What made you suspect him?

4. You are kidnapped and locked in a room with two other

people. All three of you have a number written on your foreheads. None of you know what number it is. The first man has the number 2 written on his forehead while the second man has the number 3 written on his. The kidnapper tells you that the number on one of your foreheads is the sum of the other two numbers. Each number is unique. You can't talk to each other and you cannot use sign language or any means of communication. If any of you can guess your own number, you will be set free. What number is on your forehead?

5. An elderly gentleman named Jack lived alone. Because of his old age, he couldn't leave his house. So he had everything delivered to him, including his milk, mail, newspapers and groceries. One Tuesday, the mailman went to deliver his letters and found the front door ajar. On pushing it open, he found Jack sprawled on the living-room floor, dead. He immediately called you, the police. When you arrive, you notice two bottles of milk, Monday's newspaper, a small bag of groceries, two unopened letters and some brochures on the front porch. You immediately have a suspect. Who do you arrest?

6. In a tourist village that is currently hosting gypsies, nomads, Celtic tribes and circus folk, a local shopkeeper is found dead just outside his shop. He had time to scrawl the following cryptic numbers in the sand outside before he died: 11-10-3-8-12-9. Which group do you think killed the shopkeeper?

7. Your grandfather is telling you war stories. 'At the end of World War I, I was awarded for my bravery after saving a group of my men,' he says. 'You see, we were fighting in northern France and one of our enemies threw a grenade at us. I managed to pick it up and throw it away before it exploded. So, right after the war ended, a general gave me

a sword, engraved with the words "Awarded for Bravery and Valour, A True Hero, World War I." You think about the story for a minute and then say, 'Grandpa, that story can't be true!' How do you know?

8. A man at a party was extremely thirsty and gulped down some of the freshly made iced fruit punch. Being an introvert, he left the party early. Everyone at the party who drank the fruit punch subsequently died of poisoning. Why did the man not die?

9. Margaret was found dead in her living room by Edith. Edith recounted her horrifying discovery to you, the detective on the crime scene. 'I was walking by Margaret's house when I thought I would just pop in for a visit. I noticed her living-room light on and I decided to peek in to see if she was in there. The window was fogged, so I had to wipe it to see inside. That is when I saw her body. I kicked in the front door to try and save her but she was already dead by then. I called the police immediately afterward.' You arrested Edith for murdering Margaret. How did you know that Edith was lying?

10. There are five people. One of them shot one of the five. With the help of the following clues, find out who the murderer is and who the victim is.

   • Sam ran a marathon yesterday with one of the innocent men.
   • George was a farmer before he moved to the city.
   • Ross is a top-notch computer consultant and is going to install Kevin's new computer next week.
   • The murderer had his leg amputated last month.
   • Kevin met Ricky for the first time six months ago.
   • Ricky has been in seclusion since the crime.

- Sam used to drink heavily.
- Kevin and Ross built their last computers together.
- The murderer is Ricky's brother. They grew up together.

Exercise 2: Shorthand**

The following are abbreviations of common phrases. Try and figure them out. For example, 24 H in a D may be short for '24 hours in a day'.

1. 26 L of the A
2. 7 W of the W
3. 12 S of the Z
4. 52 C in a P (W/OJs)
5. 1,000 Y in a M
6. 90 D in a R A T
7. 3 B M (S H T R)
8. 29 D in F in an L Y
9. 13 L in a B D
10. 9 L of a C

Exercise 3: Decoding Riddles!***

This is an exercise in decoding. It is twofold:

a) Using Morse code below, decode the riddles.
b) Only the riddle questions are given. Once you decode the questions, try and find an answer.

Hint: While you need analytical skills to decode the questions, the riddles themselves are downright silly and require out-of-the-box silly answers. For example, what did Cinderella wear to the beach? Glass flippers, of course!

Morse Code

A .-	K -.-	U ..-
B -...	L .-..	V ...-
C -.-.	M - -	W .- -
D -..	N -.	X -..-
E .	O - - -	Y -.- -
F ..-.	P .- -.	Z - - ..
G - -.	Q - -.-	
H	R .-.	
I ..	S ...	
J .- - -	T -	

a) . - - . . . . - . - . -/- . . - . . - - . - . -/- . - . . - - - - - - . . -/ - . - . .
. . - - . / . -/- . - . - . . - . . - - - - . - . - . . -/. . - ./ . - - - .
- . . . - . .?

b) . - - . . . . . - -/. . . . . . - . . . . - . . - . - ./- . - . . . - . . - . . . - . .
. . - . /- . . . . . . - . . - ./- - . - - - . . . ./ - - - -/. - - - .
- . . . . - . .?

c) . - - . . . . - . ./- . . - - -/- - . . - - . . - - - - - . . . ./
. . . . - - . . - -?

d) . . . . - - - . - -/. - . . . - - - - . . - - /. . . . . . . - - - . .
- . - . . . - . ./- . . - - - - . . - . - - - . . . . ./. - . - . . - .
. - - . - . - . . - . - . /- - . - . . . . . - . - . . - . .?

e) . - - . . . . . . - /. . . . . ./- . . . . /. . - . . . . - - - - . .
. . -/. - - . . - . - . - /- . - - - . . . . /. - / - . - . . . . - . - . .?

f)   . - - ... - . - -/- .. .. .. - ./- .... ./- ... .
  . - ./ ... - . . - . - ./. -/ - .. . - . - . - . -/- - - .. - ./
  . - - . .. . - . . - - . - . .. - . - - ./- . - . - . - . - . .
  . . ?

g)   . - - .... . - / .. .. ./.-/- - . .. - - ./. . - - . . - - . - - .
  . - .. - - - - . - . - - . - . . ?

h)   . - - .... . . - -/. ... . - . . ./. . - . - - - .. - . - ./. - . .
  . - - . . . . ./. - - . - . ./. . - - . . - . . . . . ?

i)   . - - .... . . - . ./- . . - - - . . . ./.-/- . - . . - - . - . .
  . - ./. . - - ?

j)   . - - .... . . - . ./- . . - - -/- . - . . - . - . ./. . . . -
  - . . - - ?

Exercise 4: Einstein's Riddle****

The following riddle is said to have been created by Albert Einstein in the last century. Einstein said that only 2 per cent of the world's population can solve it. This puzzle requires pure logic and analytical skills. All the best!

There are five houses of different colours next to each other. In each house lives a man. Each man has a unique nationality, an exclusive favourite drink, a distinct favourite brand of cigarettes and keeps a specific pet. Using all the clues below, fill up the grid and answer the question: 'Who owns the fish?'

Hint: Start with the questions that clearly state the position of the person's nationality, drink, cigarette, house colour or pet.

- The Brit lives in the red house.
- The Swede keeps dogs as pets.
- The Dane drinks tea.
- The green house is next to the white house, on the left.
- The owner of the green house drinks coffee.
- The person who smokes Pall Mall rears birds.

- The owner of the yellow house smokes Dunhill.
- The man living in the house in the centre drinks milk.
- The Norwegian lives in the first house.
- The man who smokes Blends lives next to the man who keeps cats.
- The man who keeps horses lives next to the man who smokes Dunhill.
- The man who smokes Blue Master drinks beer.
- The German smokes Prince.
- The Norwegian lives next to the blue house.
- The man who smokes Blends has a neighbour who drinks water.

	House 1	House 2	House 3	House 4	House 5
Colour					
Nationality					
Drink					
Cigarette					
Pet					

Exercise 5: Puzzle Grid****

There are two grid puzzles below. The first one is very easy and the second one is tougher. In each puzzle you are given a series of categories and an equal number of options within each category. Each option is used only once. Your goal is to figure out which options are linked together based on a series of clues. Each puzzle has only one unique solution.

The grids below allow you to cross-reference every possible option in every category. You can eliminate pairs that you know aren't true with an X, and pencil in pairs that you know are related with a √. Analyse the clues to fill up the grid.

1. Who likes Batman? Who is 10 years old?
    - Sam likes Spiderman.
    - John doesn't like Superman.
    - The youngest boy likes Spiderman.
    - The boy who likes Superman is 8 years old.

	Superheroes			Ages		
	Batman	Spiderman	Superman	6 years	8 years	10 years
Sam						
Bob						
John						

2. Mr Daley has a small carpentry shop where he carves beautiful figurines of different colours and designs every day. Last week, his theme was chess pieces. How many figurines did he make on each of the listed days and what was the colour and design of each batch?
    - The bishop-shaped figurines were not made on Tuesday. However, they were made earlier than the 700 figurines, in the same week.
    - Mr Daley made 100 more figurines in the shape of pawns than the number of yellow figurines that he made on Thursday.
    - The knight-shaped figurines were made the day before the green candles and two days before the batch of 500 orange figurines.
    - 150 more figurines in the shape of queens were made than the number of red figurines he made on Monday.

		Quantity					Colour					Design				
		450	500	600	700	750	Green	Orange	Red	White	Yellow	Bishops	Knights	Queens	Pawns	Rooks
Days	Mon															
	Tue															
	Wed															
	Thurs															
	Fri															
Design	Bishops															
	Knights															
	Queens															
	Pawns															
	Rooks															
Colour	Green															
	Orange															
	Red															
	White															
	Yellow															

analyse information quickly.

- Certain card games such as Free Cell also require some amount of strategy and planning. These games are available online.
- Buy a Rubik's Cube and try and solve it. Once you are able to solve the 3 x 3 cube easily, consider finding a 4 x 4 or even a 5 x 5 cube to solve. This helps hone your spatial abilities, eye-hand coordination and, of course, critical and analytical thinking. Try to figure out an algorithm to solve the Rubik's Cube (there are many!).
- Make mathematics fun. Analytical thinking plays a huge role in mathematics, but as grown-ups, we see little use in learning mathematical equations and other calculations that we do not need on a daily basis. Both grown-ups and kids can find enjoyment and mental challenges in math games on various websites and mobile applications.
- Solve mysteries and break codes. Reading crime stories and detective novels requires logical and analytical thinking on the part of the reader. Breaking codes and solving riddles as a hobby also helps keep the brain sharp. Try making up unique codes that only you and your friends can decipher. Try Mystery Rooms with your friends.
- Games such as sudoku and its variations include working with numbers in fun and challenging ways, and can improve the brain's ability to solve real-world problems faster.
- Rather than reacting to everyday problems, try taking time to analyse them and respond to them logically. Take time to read situations instead of reacting to them. This will reduce the overall stress in your life.
- Take a course in handwriting analysis or linguistics.

Chapter 4

Word's Worth

The limits of my language are the limits of my world.
—LUDWIG WITTGENSTEIN

Verbal reasoning is the ability to understand and logically work through concepts and problems expressed in words. At the turn of the last century, psychologists observed that there was a direct correlation between the size and strength of a person's vocabulary and the person's ability to succeed and achieve in life. In other words, people who train and develop their power of language express themselves better, and influence and inspire other people.

A strong vocabulary helps you do better in school and in your profession, as it aids your ability to think constructively, understand concepts and solve problems in logical or creative ways. Verbal reasoning tests are often used as entrance tests in schools and colleges to test an individual's aptitude. They are also used by employers as part of the recruitment process in job interviews.

The exercises in this chapter test and train your language and vocabulary as well as your ability to think and reason by working out word puzzles. They also help you hone your linguistic skills by solving verbal conundrums.

Exercise 1: Words Games*

1.   The first and last letters have been removed from the following

words. Try and find out what they are in order to complete the word.

Hint: The first and last letters are the same. For example, you can complete the word __ I L L O __ by adding a W at both ends.

a) ___ I D O ___
b) ___ H U N ___
c) ___ E D I U ___
d) ___ I V I ___
e) ___ Y P I S ___
f) ___ I T E R A ___
g) ___ O U ___
h) ___ E I N D E E ___
i) ___ O T I O ___
j) ___ O I N ___

2. Find a common word that completes the first word and begins the next word. For example, 'night ___ ___ ___ ___ boat' can be solved using the word 'life' to get 'night life' and 'life boat.'
Hint: The number of dashes is the number of letters in the word.

a) sword ___ ___ ___ ___ finger
b) sweet ___ ___ ___ ___ flake
c) play ___ ___ ___ friend
d) honey ___ ___ ___ ___ beam
e) some ___ ___ ___ ___ armour
f) cat ___ ___ ___ ___ out
g) bird ___ ___ ___ ___ less
h) free ___ ___ ___ ___ cuffed
i) sir ___ ___ ___ ___ cloth
j) over ___ ___ ___ ___ ___ less

3. All the vowels (a, e, i, o, u) have been removed from the following American states. Try and replace all of them.

a) lbm

b) clrd

c) dlwr

d) llns

e) dh

f) mn

g) nvd

h) h

i) rgn

j) txs

4. The following is a list of superheroes from the Marvel comic books and movies. Find them by striking out pairs of unnecessary letters.

a) ASJEWESFSWFSSWIFGCPOAYT JRFOBMNEREESSTH

b) SWEPSDIPODQFEUFRTJMEPAVBNWD

c) ZUWVGOPLLEDVMLEEFRUVIOINWEE

d) WDUDBIERTAEDDNBPEYOILORFLR

e) HGIEERGGOIYNTYMESABHNR

f) AFGVEDEESNOIGTYERTREFS

g) HLEUUDFKEHE RTCEBAUJGERES

h) GTBEFLSFAEHCERKEG PETAOPNRTTNBHEREETRW

i) QECURAEVPRTTTPOACVIERNUY AEDMMNEEUREDIZXCERAS

j) APWEMASDSERPVF

5. The following are word ladders created in 1878 by Lewis Carroll, the author of *Alice in Wonderland*. The object is to change one letter in every word till you reach the last word. For example, to change MICE to RATS, you would have to change MICE to MITE to MATE to MATS and finally to RATS.

Hint: All words need to be real words, not made-up words.

a) Change LIKE to MATH
LIKE

_____
_____
_____

MATH

b) Change SAIL to RUIN
SAIL

_____
_____
_____

RUIN

c) Change FOOL to SAGE
FOOL

_____
_____
_____
_____

SAGE

d) Change APE to MAN
APE

_____
_____
_____

MAN

Exercise 2: Anagram Scramble**

Unscramble the following anagrams to find out the names of different countries.

1. A infant gash
2. Sly leeches
3. Blade hangs
4. A cob maid
5. Oh it a pie
6. Adios nine
7. Bugle rum ox
8. Raga scam ad
9. Handle rents
10. No Maria

Exercise 3: Across Words**

1. Find the first two letters and the last two letters of each word.
   Hint: The last two letters of each word are the first two letters of the next word.

		C	K	S	T		

		D	U	C	T		

		U	C	A	T		

		P	R	E	S		

		L	I	T	U		

		C	L	I	N		

		I	T	I	O		

2. The following is a word pyramid. Follow the clues to fill up the blanks.

Hint: Each word has all the letters of the previous word, plus one additional letter.

a) Symbol for phosphorus
b) Never-ending mathematical value
c) Tasty baked pastry
d) Evergreen coniferous tree
e) Backbone
f) Long-billed game birds inhabiting marshy areas
g) Richly coloured viola flowers

3. The following pairs of words are opposites of each other. Figure them out and place them in the correct boxes.
   a) TTPABNSNRES

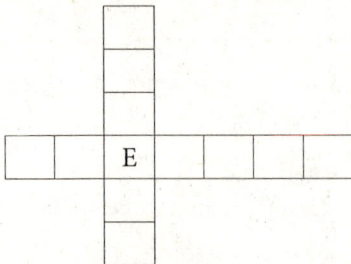

   b) NNINACTRODM

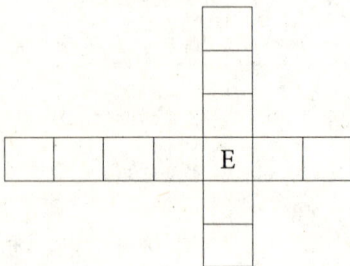

   c) VDDEELI

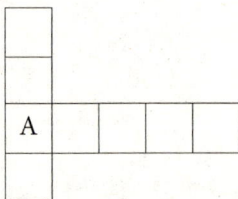

4. Unscramble the letters below to make one nine-letter word. Make as many words as you can that contain four letters and above. Each word must contain the highlighted letter. Time yourself. See if you can get over twenty words in two minutes or less for each of the words.

a)	U	Z	S	R	B	O	Z	W	D
b)	A	I	I	M	D	S	M	E	X
c)	Q	Z	N	E	G	S	I	U	E

5. Find the prefix (the word that comes before) to the following words.

   Hint: All the five words on the right have the same word on the left.

   a) ____ ____ ____ ____ ____   Conductor

   Man

   Structure

   Efficient

   Absorbent

   b) ____ ____ ____ ____ ____   Author

   Storey

   Task

   Plex

   Media

   c) ____ ____ ____ ____   Achieve

   Bearing

   Charge

   Cast

   Think

Exercise 4: Box Words***

Look at the individual boxes below and find words by starting with any letter and then moving left, right, up, down or diagonally to adjacent letters, without revisiting any square within a word. Try to find as many words as possible. There is one word that uses every letter in each box below. All words need to have four or more letters.

Hint: A minimum of 7 words, 28 words and 127 words can be found from boxes 1, 2 and 3, respectively. All words need to have four letters or more, and there must be at least one word that uses every letter in the box.

1.

G	E	D
G	Z	G
A	Z	I

2.

E	J	B	S
T	C	U	L
I	V	E	Y

3.

E	N	I	T
D	D	M	N
N	S	A	E
E	S	S	B

Exercise 5: Reverse Crossword****

The following is a crossword puzzle of school-related terms. The answers are already listed below. Enter each of the answers on the grid, one letter per square.

1.	Reading	18.	Science	35.	Educate
2.	Compass	19.	Gym	36.	Bell
3.	Spelling	20.	Blackboard	37.	Friends
4.	Classroom	21.	Recess	38.	Rulers
5.	Restrooms	22.	Eraser	39.	Music
6.	Report card	23.	Naps	40.	Sign
7.	Fees	24.	Tests	41.	Chalk
8.	Desk	25.	Geography	42.	Lab
9.	Lesson	26.	Homework	43.	Seat
10.	Mathematics	27.	Teacher	44.	Kids
11.	Case	28.	Type	45.	File
12.	Sums	29.	Art	46.	Pencil
13.	Textbooks	30.	History	47.	Neat
14.	Glue	31.	Backpacks	48.	Attendance
15.	Snacks	32.	Pens	49.	Field trip
16.	Tidy	33.	Study	50.	Binders
17.	Principal	34.	Project	51.	Students

WHAT MORE CAN YOU DO?

Verbal Reasoning (Language)

- Read. It doesn't matter what you read—just read. Make reading a habit. This is one of the biggest ways to enrich your vocabulary and improve your general knowledge.

- Watch educational documentaries and programmes. Learn the terminology used in these documentaries.

- Learn a foreign language. Watch foreign-language movies with (or without) subtitles.

- Learn a new word every day and use it at least three times in conversations. Keep a notebook of new words that you learn.

- Maintain a journal. Over time, reading it will help you examine the improvement in your writing and language skills.

- Playing games such as Scrabble, Pictionary, dumb charades, Boggle, Chinese whisper, Hangman, 20 questions, Simon Says, etc. will develop and tune your language skills.

- Making up and/or reading riddles, rhymes, tongue-twisters, lyrics to songs, poems, limericks and short stories also help in developing and training language skills. Taking part in quizzes either at work/school or online will also expand your vocabulary.

- Joining a group such as Toastmasters International and learning how to deliver dynamic speeches will not only hone your language and verbal skills but may increase your self-confidence and self-esteem as well.

Chapter 5

Loosen Up!

You can't use up creativity.
The more you use, the more you have.
—Maya Angelou

Creativity is defined as the generation of ideas or products that are both original and valuable. Creativity relies on imagination, the conscious representation of what is not immediately present to the senses. Imagination is about seeing the impossible or unreal, and creativity uses imagination to unleash and create unique and novel ideas, concepts and inventions. Creativity and imagination are the foundations of innovative thinking and hence, are tested in aptitude tests, college entrance exams and job interviews.

Creative people have the ability to devise new ways to carry out tasks, solve problems and meet challenges by bringing a fresh and sometimes unorthodox perspective to situations. Creativity is measured in terms of cognitive characteristics, such as divergent thinking (many possible solutions), convergent thinking (only one correct answer), metaphoric thinking (what if), visualization (imagery), insightful thinking, and flexibility, novelty and nonconformity in thoughts, attitudes and behaviour.

Some people are naturally more creative than others, but creative thinking can be strengthened through practice. This chapter tests and trains your creativity and imagination in fun and exciting ways.

Exercise 1: Divergent Thinking*

1. Write as many uses as you can think of for the following five common objects. Time yourself. Give yourself one minute for every word. When your time ends, tally your answers. The answers that you write down need to be as unique as possible. Obvious answers are not counted. For example, when giving the uses for a brick, answers could include using it as a paperweight, a stool, a doorstop, a weapon, a tiny table for a doll tea party, etc. An obvious answer like 'A brick can be used to build houses' will not be taken into account.

   a) A shoelace
   b) A bar of soap
   c) An empty plastic bottle
   d) A bottle of blue nail polish
   e) A fork

2. Look at the following list and see how you can associate each word with a toothbrush. You can either associate the toothbrush with something else (use both with some connection or in the same context) or see how to use the toothbrush in connection with something else. Try and find all possible uses keeping the given words in mind. Avoid obvious answers such as, 'A toothbrush can be used to brush your teeth.' Be as creative and imaginative as possible. There are no wrong answers as long as your uses for the toothbrush are plausible and can be explained.

   For example, if the required association is between a toothbrush and a doll, you could say something like, 'Cut off the head of the toothbrush and use it as a stool for the doll to sit on.' 'Or use the toothbrush as a comb for the doll's hair'.

Toothbrush	:	Headphones
	:	Newspaper
	:	Glue

:	Purse
:	Mirror
:	Car
:	Spectacles
:	Chewing gum
:	Bottle of milk
:	Television set

3. Find as many solutions as possible to the following problems. Note that the solutions need to be practical and creative at the same time.

a) How can you drop an egg from a height of 10 feet without cracking the eggshell?

b) Mr Lee's home is 5 kilometres from his office. He spends a lot of money (and time) in refuelling his car which gives him bad mileage. How can you help him save money and petrol?

c) Your sister, who is 6 years old, is having trouble concentrating on her homework. What are some ways in which you can help her focus?

d) Two of your friends are fighting over which movie to watch in the theatre. How can you help them solve this dispute?

e) You have not completed an assignment due for submission today. What are some of the excuses you can think of?

4. Make sentences with the following words, using them in different contexts. Take one minute for each word and make as many sentences as possible. For example, the word 'crane' can be used in at least three different ways, as follows: 'She had to crane her neck to see the stage better', 'That crane has a long neck!' and 'They used a crane to unload the shipping containers'.

a) Type

    b)   Rose
    c)   Leaves
    d)   Date
    e)   Engaged

5. Write down as many objects as you can think of for the following categories. Take about one minute per category.
    a)   Round objects
    b)   Noisy objects
    c)   Healthy food
    d)   Fantasy fiction movies
    e)   Popular songs that were released last year

Exercise 2: Abstract Pictures*

The images below seem like simple patterns. However, with a bit of imagination, they can become more interesting. For example, the picture to the right might just seem like an empty box, but what else do you think it can be? Maybe it's a polar bear in snow? A white painting against a white background? A close-up of a snowflake? An overexposed photograph? Take about one minute per picture and write down as many interpretations of the picture as you can think of. Avoid obvious answers.

1.

2.

3.

4.

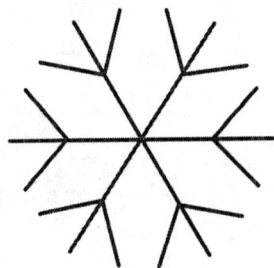

5.

6.

7.

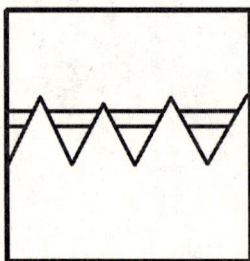

8.

9.

10.

Exercise 3: Back to the Drawing Board**

Colour the following grid to form a definite picture (not abstract). For example, here's a butterfly that has been shaded into a section of the grid. Feel free to use colour pencils, crayons or just an ordinary pencil or pen. Try and complete this exercise in 10 minutes.

[blank grid]

Exercise 4: Creative Writing***

The exercises below are to practise creative writing. All stories need to have a proper introduction, a body and a conclusion. Flesh it out when you have the time and add a plot twist (or two) to make it a complete story. You can choose any genre that you like (fantasy fiction, science fiction, horror, romance, etc.). For now, take about two to three minutes per exercise.

1. Imagine the different scenarios mentioned below and write down what you think may happen if they come true. Remember, as this is creative writing, there is no need to be scientifically accurate.

    a) What if you woke up on a strange planet?

b) What if all the scientists on Earth disappeared mysteriously?

c) What if the polar ice caps melted?

d) What if you were a dragon guarding your treasure and someone was trying to steal it?

e) What if Earth had two moons?

2. Write down micro stories following the guidelines below. The stories cannot exceed the word limit. For example, if you were told to write a micro story about the restaurant you ate at last night in not more than six words, you could try, 'I came. I ordered. I ate.'

a) Write a love story in not more than 25 words.

b) Write a horror story in not more than 15 words.

c) Write a fantasy fiction story in not more than 20 words.

d) Write an adventure story in not more than 30 words.

e) Write a cowboy western story in not more than 25 words.

3. The following are answers to riddles. Try and think of as many questions as you can that would have had the same answers. Give yourself one minute per answer.

a) A noose-paper!

b) No barking zone!

c) Lunch and dinner.

d) Meals on wheels!

e) Carps and robbers.

4. The following is a list of objects on the left and people on the right. Match three objects to three people randomly and write a short story involving all six of them. A good way to do this would be to close your eyes and randomly point to an object or a person with your pencil. Since this is an exercise on creativity and imagination, try to give the objects creative uses.

Objects		**People**	
a)	French fries	a)	Newspaper man
b)	Hairbrush	b)	Harry Potter
c)	Train	c)	Aladdin
d)	Magic wand	d)	Shopkeeper
e)	Cheese	e)	Your grandfather
f)	Rubber boots	f)	Astronaut
g)	Cup and saucer	g)	Librarian
h)	A bouquet of flowers	h)	Dracula
i)	Castle	i)	Cyclist
j)	Fangs	j)	Your boss/school principal

5. The following is a list of first lines and last lines of fictional stories. Use them to write a story of your own, making sure to start and end it with the exact words below. Your story needs to have 300 words or more. Flesh it out when you have the time. For now, take no more than five minutes for each story.

a) There was a knock on the door. 'Come in,' I said. It was the older man, the one who looked just like me ………………………………………………………………………… …………………………………………………………………………He inclined his head. It might have been a nod of agreement.

b) The path was long and deadly, but the sight that jolted me out of my reverie was far deadlier……………………… …………………………..I knew who the body belonged to. And I knew whose life he had died saving.

c) The tune sounded hauntingly familiar and yet…………… …………………………...............Without warning, the blinds closed and she was gone.

d) Marie would have to steal the diamond. What other

choice did she have? ……………...…………………
………………………...…………………………………
………………………. She'd assumed I was running a
scam and she had paid for it dearly.

e) There had to be a way to track her down. How could she
appear and disappear without a trace? …………………
……………………………………………………………
……………………………………………….……………
……………………………………….I knew she would
have wanted it that way.

Exercise 5: Black Out!***

The following is a short story titled 'The Light at the End of the
Tunnel'. It is slightly sinister in nature. Your task is to redact
words (or parts of words) or phrases in the middle so that it
transforms into a happier story. The caveat is that you cannot
add anything to the story, nor can you change it in any way
except to black out or remove words or phrases. The resulting
story doesn't have to be grammatically correct as long as it is
understandable. A brief example of blacking out words to change
a paragraph is given below:

The nagging feeling that she had somehow forgotten
something persists. She dumps the last of her suitcases into her car
and goes back inside the house. Climbing the stairs to her room,
she does a mental check of things she usually forgot. Toothbrush?
Check. Deodorant? Check. Spare pair of glasses? Check. Contact
lens solution and case? Check. She hasn't forgotten anything. Her
mom would be proud.

The nagging persists. She dumps her car Climbing the stairs
she does a check of Toothbrush?

██████ Deodorant? ██████ Spare pair of glasses? Check. Contact ████ Her mom ██████

The Light at the End of the Tunnel

He sits on the spare bed, watching her sleep. Next to her, a machine rhythmically beeps with her heartbeats. He lets out a low growl. Not long now.

In her sleep, she is dreaming. Dreaming of soaring higher and higher. Dreaming of a better life. It is a slumber that is as deep as any. It is a slumber she will never wake from.

He watches her with amusement. Tapping into her dreams is easy enough. He watches as she soars in ecstasy. Not long now, my pretty, he thinks. He quietly reaches out and touches her dream.

In her sleep, she frowns. She is in an arid desert. The heat is killing. All around for miles and miles, there is nothing but sand. She tries to fathom where civilization might be closest. South, she decides. She begins to walk. Hour after hour and still no sign of life.

All of a sudden, the dry sand in front of her cracks. The crack extends and boiling hot fumes erupt. Her skin begins to chap and peel. It's hailing. Hailing sulphur. Her skin begins to slowly burn. God help me, she cries.

He withdraws his hand in pain. Where had that come from? She is much calmer now. Hailing sulphur? Ha! She better get used to that. Where she is going, there is nothing but sulphur and heat. Loneliness and pain. He extends his hand towards her again.

She is on a raft in the middle of the ocean. Cool breeze blows through her hair. All around for miles and miles, there is nothing but water. She tries to fathom where civilization might be closest. South, she decides. She begins to row. Hour after hour and still no sign of life.

All of a sudden, a giant wave crashes into her raft. She is immediately hit by another wave on the opposite side. The sea that was calm just a minute ago is suddenly roiling and churning. The water becomes fire. Flames engulf her. Batter her. Consume her. Her skin begins to burn and char. The pain is excruciating. God help me, she cries.

He withdraws his hand in agony. Funny how fire soothes and yet the one name he was terrified of can burn. He watches, silently, as her dreams return to normal. She looks peaceful. The end is not far, he smirks. What you saw was just a whiff of your new home. Enjoy the calm while you can.

It is time. The end is not far. The beginning is close. The machine by her bed begins to beep at faster intervals. He extends his hand once more.

She is on a grassy mountain. Multicoloured butterflies flit about her. The mountains look inviting. She would love to see the world from the top. She begins to climb. Hour after hour and still not nearer to the top. She decides to rest awhile.

She sits on a boulder. All of a sudden, the boulder shifts and she is in a cave. The cave is pitch black. She is not alone. Gossamer wings lightly touch her and move on. Somewhere overhead, a bat screeches. A quiet voice whispers: it's not too late to get out. Get out of the cave. The tunnel. Go back to the butterflies on the mountain slopes. Don't walk towards the light.

The light? A ray slices through the darkness. She ignores the voice and continues walking. It is easy for her to do so. She's been ignoring that voice all her life.

He is there, walking beside her. Leading her.

The ray thickens and widens. Beckons, almost. He stops in the darkness. Rules are rules. It's still not too late. The choice is hers to make. Brilliant light or grassy mountains?

She turns and, for an eternity, gazes at the dark tunnel behind her and the peaceful plains beyond. She turns and looks at the brilliant light ahead. He holds his breath. She is still uncertain.

The machine beeps in staccatos. Faster and faster. And suddenly deadpans a single eternal beep. She is free now. Free to make her decision. In the darkness behind her, he watches. Watches as she chooses her fate. Her destiny.

He knows that all that awaits her on the other side is oblivion. Brimstone, sulphur and fire make the light brilliant. Mortals always had a flair for romanticizing the deadly. Stupid mortals. Believing that the light at the end of the tunnel was their reward for being good. Stupid, stupid mortals.

She takes an unsteady step towards the light. Her next step is more certain. Hadn't mamma always talked about moving towards the light? She is more certain now. She has made her choice. She begins to walk faster.

And in the darkness behind her, he smiles.

WHAT MORE CAN YOU DO?

Creativity and Imagination

- Don't accept, ask. Keep questioning things around you. Don't take anything for granted. Question conventions, beliefs, thinking patterns, science (the list is exhaustive!), etc. Find inspiration everywhere.
- Find time for a hobby. A hobby, such as playing a musical instrument, running or collecting memorabilia, can help you relax and fight stress, along with boosting creativity.
- Role-playing board games such as Dungeons and Dragons, Pathfinder Pawns, etc; role-playing video games such as The Witcher, World of Warcraft, Pillars of Eternity, Skyrim,

Fallout, etc., and game applications that can be downloaded on mobile phones such as Minecraft, Big Brain Academy, Terraria, Dragon Ninja Rush, Little Big Planet, Portal, etc. also enhance creativity and imagination.

- Unplug your phone, computer and other gadgets for half an hour to an hour every day. Gadgets have the ability to stunt your creativity and imagination, since they provide the visuals for you. Being addicted to your phone will definitely reduce your creativity and productivity. It's okay to let go of gadgets and unplug yourself from the Internet at least for a few minutes (to begin with) every day.
- Set a time for social media. It is not necessary to constantly check your social media accounts every time you get a notification or when you're bored. Try to limit your time on social media to just fifteen minutes in the morning and at night.
- Use the Six Thinking Hats Technique to look at every problem from six perspectives. This will keep you productive while creatively solving an issue that is stressing you out.
- Take time to doodle or draw something every day. Try and draw with both hands at the same time. Whether your drawing is good or not, this simple activity will stimulate the right hemisphere of your brain, which is also the creative side.
- Make something new, funny or weird with objects lying around your house.
- Rather than showing people photographs, try and describe your holiday (or whatever you had photographed) to them.
- Do nothing. Have one 'Do Nothing Day' in a month, where you can stay home with absolutely no agenda and no plan and simply be. Our daily lives are filled with so much hustle and bustle that it becomes difficult to find time for ourselves.

Having a 'Do Nothing Day' can help balance out this stress.

- Pick a song that you like, and try and sing it with your own lyrics. Look at clouds and imagine them as things. Build something fun with Legos. Substitute ingredients in recipes. Imagine alternative endings to your favourite movies and stories. Try and do your normal chores with a creative twist.

Chapter 6

Figure It Out

Pure mathematics is, in its own way,
the poetry of logical ideas.
—ALBERT EINSTEIN

Numerical reasoning is the ability to deal with numbers quickly and accurately. Numerical reasoning tests not only test and train your basic mathematical abilities but also your ability to use numerical data as a tool to make reasoned decisions and solve problems. These tests contain questions that assess your knowledge of percentages, number sequences and data interpretation, and make use of your logic and analytical skills.

Numerical reasoning questions are present in all aptitude tests. Studies indicate that people who train this area of cognition are more confident in their interpersonal interactions, faster at solving real-world problems and more likely to tackle stressful situations with a solution-focused approach.

This chapter contains five main exercises in numerical reasoning, only a few of which require mathematical calculations. The rest of the exercises require manipulation of numbers in a logical sequence or placement of numbers (or shading of boxes or drawing lines) according to pre-established rules. Even though the difficulty level keeps increasing with every exercise and sometimes within each exercise itself, work out the logic behind the exercises and attempt all of them. If you are stuck, take a peek at the answer at the end, but work out the remaining exercise by yourself. Do not attempt all the questions at once. Take a break between exercises so that you do not overwork your brain.

Exercise 1: Simple Math*

1. What percentage of this grid is black and what percentage is white?

2. Which is the lower figure—the square root of 3 or the cube root of 5?
3. In a deck of playing cards, what is the sum of all the number cards?
4. Which of the following numbers are not prime numbers?
   3   13   23   33   73   113   143   173
5. Which three consecutive numbers can be multiplied to equal 1716?
6. Fill in the boxes in this mini sudoku so that each row and each column have the numbers 1, 2, 3 and 4 in them without repeating any number. The darker 2 x 2 boxes also need to have all four numbers in them without repeating any number.

		2	4
4	3		

7. The number of pairs of socks in a drawer is between 50 and 60. If you count them 3 at a time, you will find that there are 2 pairs left over. If you count them 5 at a time, you will find that there are 4 pairs left over. How many pairs of socks are there in the drawer?

8. Sophie works every second day at a supermarket and Stephie works every third day at the same supermarket. The supermarket is open on all seven days of the week. This week, Sophie started work on Tuesday, 1 December, and Stephie started work on Wednesday, 2 December. On what day will both of them work together next?

9. What number comes next?

   852 : 42
   756 : 36
   469 : ?

10. One number from the top needs to replace one number from the bottom and vice versa. Which two numbers in the two sequences below need to be swapped? What is the logic behind the sequence?

    20, 19, 17, 16, 14, 12
    20, 18, 17, 15, 14, 13

Exercise 2: Deadly Sequences**

Look at the sequences below and logically deduce what number replaces the question mark at the end.

Hint: Each question makes use of a different logical sequence.

1. 8723, 3872, 2387, ?
2. 35, 57, 86, 25, 756, 65, 75, 26, 875, ?
3. 25, 10, 35, 15, 50, ?, ?
4. 237 (13), 349 (21), 826 (?)
5. 440, 436, 433, 430, 427, ?

6. 27, 82, 41, 124, 62, 31, 94, 47, 142, 71, ?, ?
7. 77, 143, 221, 323, ?
8. 8, 12, 24, 60, ?
9. 1, 5, 32, 288, ?
10. 6, 9, 27, 54, ?, 2241

Exercise 3: Questioning Question Marks**

1. What number should replace the question mark?

634	97
543	?

2. What number should replace the question mark?

5	5
5	2

6	8
7	5

?	7
6	4

3. What letters should replace the question marks?

B	X
D	V
?	?
H	R
J	P
L	N

4. What number should replace the question mark?

9		7
	5	
6		5

8		8
	3	
4		9

7		4
	6	
3		?

5. What number should replace the question mark?

| 20 | 27 | 36 |

| 4 | 3 | 6 |

| 5 | 9 | ? |

6. What number should replace the question mark?

| 5 | 7 |
| 2 | 78 |

| 3 | 6 |
| 61 | 4 |

| 1 | ? |
| 8 | 9 |

| 29 | 4 |
| 2 | 3 |

7. What number should replace the question mark?

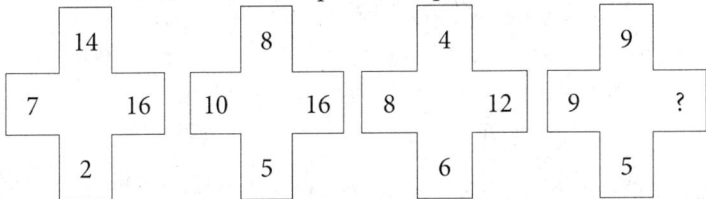

	14	
7		16
	2	

	8	
10		16
	5	

	4	
8		12
	6	

	9	
9		?
	5	

8. The top set of six numbers has a relationship with the set of six numbers below. By working out the relationship of the block of numbers to the left, try and figure out what numbers should replace the question marks on the right.

2	5	4	9	8	3		13	26	19	32	23	18
1	6	3	10	7	4		?	?	?	?	?	?

9. What number should replace the question mark?

1	2	3
	9	
5	6	7

6	7	8
	2	
1	7	2

2	3	4
	2	
6	7	9

?	6	8
	1	
7	7	2

10. The two sets of nine numbers relate to each other in a certain way. Work out the missing numbers on the right by working out the logic behind the numbers on the left.

3	7	9
4	3	1
8	1	0

5	7	6
?	?	?
9	0	5

Exercise 4: Placement Puzzles***

Placement puzzles may ask you to shade in squares, draw lines to form pathways, draw outlines or place numbers in a grid in a logical sequence. While these puzzles do not require any particular mathematical calculations, they do require precision, logic and analytical thinking. Take a few minutes to understand the puzzles and what is required of you before attempting them.

1. **Nonogram:** Shade in some squares on the grid on the right following the clues given on the outside. Each number depicts the number of consecutive squares that need to be shaded in that particular row or column. For example, if the number at the top is 2, it means that that column has 2 consecutively shaded squares. If the number on the side is 4, it means that that particular row has 4 consecutively shaded squares.

	2	4	6	8	10	4	4	4	4	4
1										
2										
3										
9										
10										
10										
9										
3										
2										
1										

2. **Pathways:** Fill the grid below with numbers from 1 to 64 so that each number forms a path within the grid, visiting each box only once. The numbers can be placed horizontally, vertically or diagonally in any direction.

					5	9	
		59	1		19		
	63			20			12
36			32			17	
			55		23		14
39		42		54			15
			53			29	
44				51		26	

3. **Reverse minesweeper:** The clues in the following puzzle tell you the number of mines surrounding it. For example, if the number is 2, it means that there are two mines in the adjacent squares surrounding the number 2. You need to either shade in the mines or mark them with an X.

   Hint: There might be a few blank squares as well (squares that don't have mines or numbers).

	1			1			1		
2		2		2				2	
	3		2		1	2			
		2		2			2		1
			1						1
				3			1		
		2		3		2			
	4				2			2	
2			4	2			2		
		2						4	

4. **Infinite lines:** The puzzle on the right is similar to reverse minesweeper. The numbers in the boxes depict how many surrounding boxes have lines running through them. You need to draw a single line through some of the empty boxes (lines cannot pass through numbered boxes) so that the line does not cross or overlap in any way. Lines can be either vertical or horizontal. A simple example has been provided.

						5		3
				6				
		8			4			
5								
							4	
			4		3			

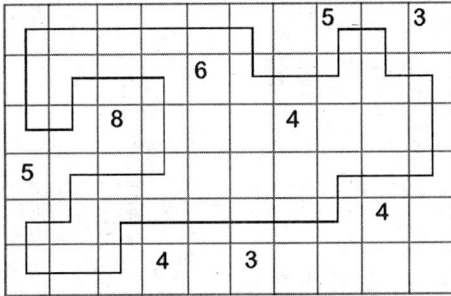

				3	2	4		
		7						
4		7		6		8		
								5
					7			
	5		7				6	
	5						4	
			7			5		
			4					

5. **Carpeting:** The following puzzle requires you to 'carpet' the area of the grid that is represented by specific numbers by shading in the required boxes. For example, if the number is 2, then two boxes (including the box with the number)

need to be shaded. The catch is that only boxes that form rectangles or squares can be shaded—irregular shapes cannot be shaded. Also, no two 'carpets' can overlap. For example, Figure 1 below is wrong, while Figure 2 is correct.

Hint: There can be blank boxes between carpets.

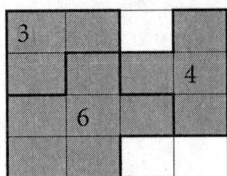

Figure 1

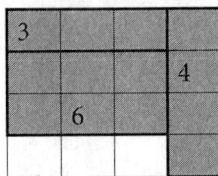

Figure 2

3			3			4		
		3				1		3
			2	3	2			
2	3		4					4
			5			4		
	4		2					
			6		3		3	
				3	2			6
		4						
3	2				3		6	

Exercise 5: Grid Puzzles****

Grid puzzles require mathematical calculations, logic and analytical thinking. Take time to understand the puzzle before attempting it.

1. The grid below is a magic square that equals 264. This means that not only should each row and column add up to 264, but each corner 2 × 2 grid within the larger square also needs to add up to 264.

    Hint: The two diagonal lines that crisscross the square also equal 264! Two numbers are given to help you get started.

96			
			81

2. **Kakuro:** Kakuro puzzles are often referred to as number crosswords. The aim is to fill all the blank squares in the grid with only the numbers from 1 to 9 so that the numbers you enter add up to the corresponding clues.

    Kakuro puzzles contain many clue squares, which help you solve the puzzle. A clue square can have an 'across' clue or a 'down' clue, or both. The across clue is the number that is on the top right corner and the down clue is the number on the bottom left corner. The aim is to fill up the squares adjacent to the across clue with numbers that add up to the clue and to fill up the squares below the down clue so that the numbers add up to the clue.

For example, look at the sample puzzle below. As you can see, the number 9 is the 'down' clue and therefore all the numbers below number 9 need to add up to 9. Number 4 is the 'across' clue, which means that all the numbers adjacent to the clue have to add up to number 4. Numbers within a block must not repeat. For example, the numbers that add up to number 9 cannot be 7 + 1 + 1.

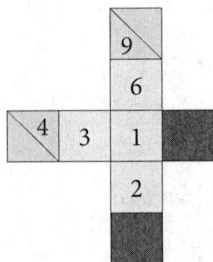

Try working out the following kakuro puzzle in 20 minutes or less.

Hint: Start with a clue for which you know the answer to some certainty. For example, if the clue is number 3, you know that the adjacent two squares can only have two options of 2 + 1 or 1 + 2.

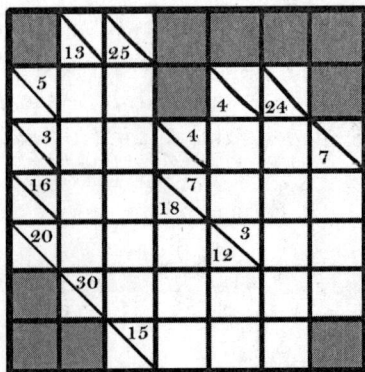

3. **Sudoku:** Technically, a sudoku is a placement puzzle as it involves placing numbers in a grid and no mathematical calculations. However, we will include it in the category of grid puzzles, because of the sheer complexity involved in solving it. Don't let the complexity of the puzzle fool you, all you need is cold, hard logic to solve it.

    You have already worked out a mini sudoku in Exercise 1, Question 6, of this chapter. The following is a larger 10 x 10 grid with smaller, irregular 10-cell grids within. Your task is to make sure that you fill in all numbers from 0 to 9 in each row, each column, as well as the smaller outlined 10-cell grids so that the numbers are not repeated in the same row, column or grid. An example is given below.

5	1	0	9	7	8	2	4	6	3
2	4	9	3	0	6	1	5	7	8
6	7	3	8	4	1	5	2	0	9
3	8	7	0	5	9	6	1	4	2
0	6	8	4	2	3	7	9	1	5
9	2	4	6	1	5	3	7	8	0
1	5	2	7	9	0	8	6	3	4
8	0	5	1	6	2	4	3	9	7
4	3	1	2	8	7	9	0	5	6
7	9	6	5	3	4	0	8	2	1

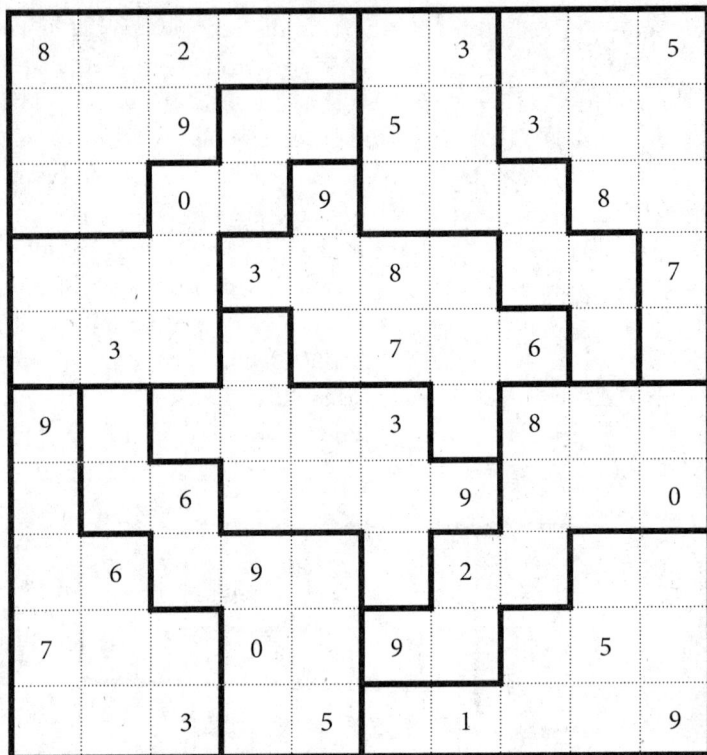

WHAT MORE CAN YOU DO?

Numerical Reasoning

- Games such as Battleship, Tic Tac Toe, Connect Four, Breakout, Chinese chequers, chess, etc., which require logic and reasoning, also improve numerical reasoning.
- Mathematical board games for early learners include Achi, Robot Turtles, Qwirkle, Set, Ice Cool, Tsuro, etc.

- Mathematical board games for kids aged 8 and above include Dara, Suspend, Reversi, Ticket to Ride, Laser Khet 2.0, Loony Quest, Ricochet Robots, etc.
- Mathematical board games for older children and adults include Love Letter, Escape from the Aliens in Outer Space, Splendor, Five Tribes, Sagrada, Prime Climb, Telepathy, Settlers of Catan, Straw, City of Zombies, Clue, Camel Up, Stone Age, etc.
- Try and work out crosswords, sudoku, futoshiki, kuromasu, calcudoku, maze puzzles, fillomino, slitherlink, kakuro, masyu, linesweeper, etc. on a daily basis. These puzzles keep your brain sharp and focused, and improve your concentration as well as your numerical abilities. Understand the concept of the puzzle before you begin.
- When working out puzzles, time yourself and see how quickly and accurately you can complete a puzzle.
- Apply mathematics to real life. Try doing everyday transactions and calculations mentally without using calculators.
- Practise! Practise! Practise! Review errors and see how to correct them.

Chapter 7

Out of the Box

Rightness is what matters in vertical thinking.
Richness is what matters in lateral thinking.
—EDWARD DE BONO

The term 'lateral thinking' was coined by Dr Edward de Bono in 1967. Lateral thinking is also called abstract reasoning, which tests your ability to solve problems in creative, imaginative and unique or out-of-the-box ways. Lateral-thinking problems require systematic but creative solutions, which can be obtained by attempting to look at the problem from many different perspectives, rather than by looking for a direct solution.

In this chapter, we will take a break from logical, analytical and mathematical thinking and focus on lateral thinking. While some of the problems may look logical and straightforward, remember that the obvious solution may not always be the correct one. To solve all the questions in this section, it is necessary to think laterally and creatively, and to look for solutions that may not seem obvious at first. Some puzzles may have alternative reasonable solutions than the ones listed in this book, while other puzzles will have only one possible answer.

If you do not know the answer to a particular question, resist the urge to look it up. Instead, shelve it for the time being and come back to it later. If you look at the answers immediately, you are not giving your brain time to be creative and think of possible solutions.

Examples of lateral thinking problems:
1. What word replaces the question mark?
   Onerously, honeymoon, pioneered, wagonette, ?
   a) erroneous
   b) milestone
   c) stonewall
   d) prisoner
   e) woebegone
2. If HALT = 10, LINK = 9 and TAXI = 8, what value does FAIL have?
3. You see a boat filled with people. You blink and look again, but this time you don't see a single person on the boat. Why?
   Hint: The boat has not sunk.

Answers:
1. The answer is prisoner. In the question, the word 'one' moves to the right in each successive word. Therefore, the sequence is one******, *one******, **one****, ***one*** and ****one**(prisoner).
2. FAIL = 9. The numbers indicate the number of straight lines in each word.
3. All the people on the boat are married, none of them are 'single'.

Did you get any of the answers right? Now that you've had a taste of lateral-thinking puzzles, go ahead and try out the rest of the puzzles in this chapter. Remember to let your creativity and imagination loose and look at the problems from as many perspectives as you can.

Exercise 1: Brain-Teasers*

1. Thanks to an anonymous call, the police raid a house to arrest an alleged murderer. They don't know what he looks like, but they know that his name is Victor and that he is in the house. The police find four people playing poker: one is a carpenter, one is a truck driver, one is a car mechanic and the last is an electrical engineer. They go straight to the electrical engineer and say, 'Victor, you are under arrest!' How did they know who he was?

2. A widower king has no heir. He must decide who will reign after he dies. He decides to have a contest. He gives all the children of the kingdom a single seed each. Whichever child has the largest, most beautiful plant at the end of the contest will earn the throne and be the king or queen in future. At the end of the contest, all the children present their gigantic, beautiful plants to the king. However, the king chooses a little girl with an empty pot to be the next queen. What makes him decide this?

3. In a little village, there are two barbershops, each with one barber. They are situated at opposite sides of the village. The barbershop located in the posh part of the town is tastefully decorated, neat and clean. The barber himself is a hospitable man with a ready smile, always dressed well, with his hair styled neatly, shoes polished and clothes immaculate. The barbershop on the poorer side of the town is dilapidated and shabby. The barber himself is grumpy, always frowning, dressed sloppily with his hair greased back, shoes scuffed and clothes in tatters. A visiting tourist hears of both the barbershops but decides to go to the grumpy, sloppily dressed barber in the poor part of the town. Why does he do this?

4. A man works at an aquarium that has a variety of fish and

numerous fish tanks. His job is to maintain all the fish tanks in the aquarium but finds that he spends most of his time asking people to stop tapping on the glass in the shark tank. He is falling behind on his work and so he comes up with an innovative solution. The next day, not a single person taps on the glass, but he is fired from his job. What solution do you think he came up with?

5. In a land far away, it was common knowledge that if you drank poison, the only way to save yourself was to drink a stronger poison, which would neutralize the weaker poison. The king of the land wanted to own the strongest poison known to man so that he could survive any assassination (by poisoning) attempt. So he called his researcher and doctor and gave each of them a week to make the strongest poison known to man. At the end of the week, each of them would drink the other's poison and then his own. The survivor would obviously be the one who had the stronger poison.

   The researcher went straight to work, but the doctor was cunning and devised a plan to survive while making sure that the researcher would die. When the researcher noticed that the doctor wasn't working on the poison, he guessed that he must have come up with a devious plan. He thought for a while and then came up with a counter plan to make sure that he would survive while the doctor would die.

   At the end of the week, the king summoned both of them. As planned, both the researcher and the doctor drank the other's poison first and then their own. The doctor died, the researcher survived and the king did not get what he wanted. What do you think happened?

6. At a pub, a man is running low on money. He sees the man next to him pull out a wad of ₹2,000 notes from his wallet. He turns to the rich man and says, 'Do you know something?

I have an amazing talent. I know every song that has ever existed! In fact, I bet you all the money in your wallet that I can sing a genuine song that contains a lady's name of your choice in it!'

The rich man laughs heartily and says, 'Okay then, my daughter's name is Sriranjini Shivakumari Dasagupta. Let's hear you sing that "genuine" song with her name in it now.'

Everybody in the pub listens in awed silence as the man immediately belts out the song. The rich man loses the bet and goes home with an empty wallet and the poor man goes home rich.

I bet you know this song too. Can you guess what song the man sang?

7. A young lady was having lunch with her friends at a restaurant when she noticed an elderly woman, sitting a few tables from her, staring at her. Just before she left, the elderly woman approached her and said, 'I'm sorry if I made you uncomfortable by staring at you so much. You see, you look exactly like my daughter when she was your age and she passed away last month. Would you do me a small favour, please?' Intrigued, the young lady agreed. The elderly woman continued, 'As I leave the restaurant, would you be kind enough to wave and say "goodbye mother" to me? It would warm my heart to be called "mother" again.' The young lady agreed and as requested, waved goodbye to the elderly woman while calling out 'goodbye mother!' to her. Soon after that, she received the shock of her life. Can you guess what it was?

8. A school principal was on his rounds to check if the teachers were doing their jobs diligently. He was very impressed with one teacher in particular. He noticed that every time she asked a question, every child in her class would raise their

hands enthusiastically to answer. More surprising, however, was the fact that while the teacher chose a different child each time, the child always answered correctly. He wouldn't be as impressed if he knew the secret. Can you figure it out?

9. Jack and his friend Thomas loved challenging each other for various tasks. One day, Jack surprised Thomas by saying, 'I can answer any question in the world. Go ahead. Try me. If I fail to answer any question, you can choose any penalty for me.' Thomas accepted this challenge and wrote down a list of impossibly difficult questions for Jack to answer. Unbelievably, Thomas lost the bet as Jack indeed answered all the questions! How do you think Jack won?

10. A nasty king went pillaging in a nearby village for slaves to serve him. He decided that if any villager had more than five children, he would take them as slaves. He came to the hut of a poor cobbler who had ten children. When the king came to take them, the cobbler and his wife begged him to spare them, for they were all very young. Finally, the king said, 'I see you have ten pairs of shoes in a box. If you can give each of your children a pair and still have one pair left in the box, you can keep all your children.' The cobbler and his wife were terrified at first but then smiled at each other as they had found the solution. How do you think they saved all their children?

Exercise 2: Riddles*

The following are riddles that require out-of-the-box answers. Read the questions carefully before answering.

1. A king, a queen and two twins lay in a large room, yet there was nobody there. How is this possible?
2. Four people go out for lunch and share a large pizza. They

divide it into equal parts with five straight cuts and each gets three pieces. How?

3. It is estimated that the Earth weighs 6 sextillion tons. How much more would the Earth weigh if 1 sextillion tons of concrete and stone were used to build a wall?

4. Our basketball team won a game last week with the score of 75-70, and yet not even one man in our team scored a single point. How is that possible?

5. A child playing on the beach has 4 sand piles in one area and 5 in another. If he puts them all together, how many sand piles will he have?

6. A legendary athlete was such a fast runner that his friends said he could switch off the light and jump into bed before the room got dark. On one occasion, he actually proved he could do it. How?

7. One day, Mrs Malcom's earrings fell into her cup of coffee, yet they did not get wet. How is this possible?

8. While on safari in the wild jungles of Africa, Dr Desmond woke up one morning and felt something in the back pocket of her shorts. It had a head and a tail but no legs. When she got up, she could feel it move inside her pocket. However, she didn't bother about it and went about her morning rituals. Why did she have such a casual attitude towards the thing in her pocket?

9. The day before yesterday I was 25 years old, but next year, I will be 28 years old. When is my birthday?

10. How many seconds are there in a year? (Don't use a calculator for this one!)

Exercise 3: Lateral Sequencing**

Complete the following sequences and replace the question marks with the appropriate letter or number. While these questions may remind you of the sequences that you worked out in the last chapter, remember that these are not mathematical questions and do not need hard-core logic or mathematics to be solved.

1. If 8080 = 6, 8081 = 5, 8181 = 4, then 8000 = ?
2. 2, 4, 6, 30, 32, 34, 36, 40, 42, 44, 46, 50, 52, 54, 56, 60, 62, 64, 66, ?
3. O, T, T, F, F, S, S, ?
4. N, U, S, J, M, E, V, ?
5. Which letter (not number) replaces the question mark?
   023, 790, 74933, 8019, 81?3
6.

7.

8. What is the next figure in this odd sequence? Outline it on the grid.

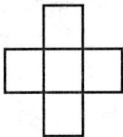

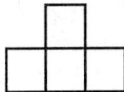

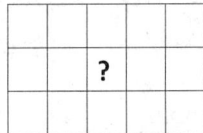

9. Z, X, C, V, B, ?
10. A, K, Q, J, T, N, E, ?

Exercise 4: Rebus**

The following words are used in different orientations to represent common phrases. Try to figure them out. For example, 'Busines' can be interpreted as 'unfinished business' and 'PAWALKRK' can be interpreted as 'walk in the park'.

1. FLIGHTFLIGHT
2. A4ID
3. THAT IS
4. GIVE GIVE GIVE GIVE GET GET GET GET
5. B B
    A A
    R R
    S S
6. SGEG
7. MOUNT MOUNT MOUNT MOUNT MOUNT
    MOUNT MOUNT MOUNT MOUNT MOUNT
8. KNEE
    LIGHTS
9. YYYMEN
10. SPIBRED

Exercise 5: Divergent Superstitions**

The following is a list of common superstitions. Your task is to write as many stories as you can think of for each superstition, with your own interpretation of their origins. Your stories can be as long as you want. Make them as creative and outlandish as possible. Even if you know the real background to some of these superstitions, try and come up with your own.

For example, if the superstition is 'never cross the road after a black cat has crossed it', I might write a story about how I had an accident when a black cat suddenly ran across the road and took me by surprise, or how a black cat walked through oil and had crossed the road with oily paws and everyone else who crossed after it slipped and slid their way across the road. Ever since, it was considered bad luck to cross the road after a black cat.

1. Never walk under a ladder.

2. Breaking a mirror will give you seven years of bad luck.
3. If you drop it, toss a pinch of salt over your left shoulder to avoid bad luck.
4. Never open an umbrella inside the house.
5. Always say 'god bless you' when someone sneezes.
6. A rabbit's foot will bring you good luck.
7. Four-leafed clovers are good luck.
8. Always wish upon a falling star.
9. Always hold your breath while crossing a graveyard.
10. It is unlucky for a bridegroom to see his bride in her wedding dress before the wedding.

WHAT MORE CAN YOU DO?

Lateral Thinking

- Don't limit your thinking to what you already know. Expand your thinking by interacting with a wide variety of people, reading a variety of books, journals and magazines, and watching a wide range of movies and documentaries.
- Never think that resources and solutions are finite or limited. There are always solutions available around you. You just have to tap into them.
- Try and use analogies and metaphors in your speech and writing. Make sure that these are original and not clichéd.
- Create a mind map when you are studying or brainstorming.
- Place yourself in someone else's shoes and see how they might solve a particular problem. For example, if Mahatma Gandhi was in my position, what would he do? Or if I were to see this problem from Mahatma Gandhi's point of view or through his eyes, what would I do differently?

- Practise stream-of-consciousness writing. This is a free-flow exercise where you write down whatever comes to mind without stopping or judging it.
- Practise reverse thinking. Think of what people would do and then do the opposite.
- Create and develop lateral-thinking habits that produce great results. Keep it simple.

Chapter 8

Stop, Look and Listen!

People's minds are changed through
observation and not through argument.
—WILL ROGERS

Active observation is the foundation of memory and learning. For any information to enter your awareness, you need to observe it first. Observation need not just include sight, but it should also be inclusive of other senses, such as sound, taste, touch and smell. At any given time, we are taking in information through our senses but we are aware of only a fraction of this information. When we actively observe our environment, we make use of all our senses to absorb information and expand our awareness of the surroundings. For example, as you read this, can you extend your awareness to sounds in your environment that you had previously ignored? Can you feel the texture of the page/device against your fingers? Can you now smell something that was not in your awareness just a moment ago? Congratulations! You are now actively observing your environment!

Since active observation involves most or all of your senses, it is an exercise that activates your entire brain. Active observation helps you remember information better, pay attention to and notice intricate details of the world around you. It assists in making you a better listener, honing your focus and concentration skills, improving your deduction skills as well as your critical-thinking skills, helping you read body language better and also helping you enjoy unusual things around you that may skip others' attention. Individuals who hone their observation skills have a broader perspective of the world around them. They are able to solve problems better and have an eye for detail.

This chapter is going to be slightly different from all the other chapters in this book. It will have only two exercises that involve filling answers, the rest of the exercises include honing your five senses, playing observation games with friends or family or just going out and putting your skills to the test. Have fun with these exercises and try to make active observation a large part of your everyday life.

Exercise 1: Training Your Senses*

In this exercise, we will start with a mindfulness technique to help you be more aware of your five senses. We will then move on to a technique to ground yourself, which will help you focus better and stop your mind from wandering. We will then end with an observation exercise for all the five senses.

Wear comfortable, loose clothing. Sit on a chair, in an upright position with your feet flat on the ground and your palms on your thighs or on your desk. While doing these exercises, try to suspend any kind of meaning or judgement that you usually place on things or people around you. Try to block out your thoughts. Instead, focus on your breathing and your sense of sight, touch, smell, hearing and taste. If you find your mind wandering, gently remind yourself to come back to the present moment.

It is recommended that you do each of the following three exercises at different times during the day or on three different days.

1. Five Senses Awareness

The aim of this exercise is to activate each of your five senses one by one and to bring awareness to each of them. This exercise can also be used to calm yourself down when you are feeling stressed, upset, anxious or nervous about something. You can spend as much time as you like on each of your senses but keep a minimum of one minute for each.

Sight: While remaining seated and focusing on your breathing, gently turn your head and scan your surroundings from left to right. Take time to look at the colours, shapes and textures of each object in your line of vision. Can you see dust on certain objects? Notice things that are in your peripheral vision (not directly in front of you) without moving your eyes. Do you see things you had not noticed before? You may close your eyes for the remaining exercises if you wish (after reading through what needs to be done). It might help you focus better on your other senses.

Sound: Begin noticing the sounds around you. You don't have to identify the sounds—simply notice them. Are there some sounds within your body that you can hear? Can you hear your own breathing? Can you hear the birds in the trees? Or the wind? Can you hear the sound of traffic? Can you hear music being played from a few houses away? Or the sound of people talking somewhere in the distance? Is there a sound that has been there but is just now entering your awareness? Is there a sound that is so soft that it is barely audible?

Smell: Shift your attention to the smells in your surroundings. Can you smell your own perfume or deodorant? Is there food being cooked right now in your kitchen? Can you smell it? If you are outside, is there a fragrance of flowers, leaves or trees around you? Can you smell freshly dug-up earth? Going by your sense of smell alone, do you think it might rain today? What makes you think that? Can you smell the paper in the book that you are holding?

Touch: Bring your attention to the sensations that you feel with your body. Can you feel the chair that you are sitting on? Can you feel the texture of the clothes that you are wearing? Or the jewellery that you may be wearing? Do they feel soft, hard, smooth or rough? Can you feel the pressure of your feet on the floor? How does the floor feel—cool, hot, wet, dirty? What is the temperature of your surroundings and how does it make you feel? Is it humid, cold, wet, dry? Are your clothes or hair moving?

Taste: Move your attention to your sense of taste. If you are currently eating something, pay attention to its texture, taste and how it feels in your mouth. Take time to chew each bite, making sure to focus on its taste. If you are not currently eating, notice if there is an aftertaste to the food that you had previously eaten or something that you had previously drunk. Bring your attention to your tongue as well as your saliva. Run your tongue along your teeth and cheeks, and notice their texture and taste.

Slowly bring your attention back to your breathing and open your eyes. Take a moment to notice how your body feels right now, in this moment. Compare how you were feeling before you started this exercise. Has anything changed? Carry this new awareness with you for the rest of the day.

2. Grounding

Grounding is also called centering. It is good to centre yourself just before starting an important task—a meeting, class or an exam—so that you block out all distraction and focus only on the task at hand. Grounding also helps during panic attacks and stressful situations. It helps you focus on your immediate environment by noticing and observing various things. All that is needed in this exercise is to notice something that you are experiencing with each of your five senses. Follow the same order given below.

Notice five things that you can see. Slowly scan your environment from left to right. Try and find five objects that are very different from each other. Focus on each of the five objects individually. Notice their shapes and colours.

Notice four things that you can feel. Bring your awareness to four things that you are currently able to touch or four things that are touching you. It can be anything from the texture of your clothes, to the sensation of the breeze on your skin, or the smooth surface of the chair you are sitting on.

Notice three things that you can hear. Bring all the sounds in your environment to your awareness. Is your fan making a noise? Can you hear your neighbour's pressure cooker whistling? Can you hear birds chirping?

Notice two things that you can smell. Shift your awareness to the smells around you. It does not matter if they are pleasant or unpleasant. Try and pick out two distinct smells from your environment and identify them.

Find one thing that you can taste and focus on it. You can take a sip of water or juice if you prefer, eat a chocolate or just be aware of the current taste in your mouth.

3. Observation Exercise

Strengthening your observation skills involves making sure all your senses are tuned in to your environment. Here are a few exercises to help you train your five senses of sight, touch, sound, taste and smell.

Sight: Though we don't realize it, most of us focus only on a few things in our environment, while everything else is ignored. These days, we have our eyes glued to our cell phones and sometimes even things that are immediately in front of us are ignored. Here are two observation exercises that you can try, to help hone your visual observation skills.

a) Straw and toothpick exercise: This exercise can be done at home. Place any object in front of you to focus on. The object can be anything from a book to a bottle of water or a vase. Place the object about four to five feet in front of you (not too close) and look directly at it. Now, without looking away from the object, try and determine how far left or right you can see (peripheral vision). Place a cup with a straw inside it on the edge of your reach, on your left hand side. Again, without taking your eyes off the main object or moving your head in any way, try to stick a toothpick into the hole in the straw. Repeat this exercise on the right-hand side.

Keep practising this method every day, trying to move the cup with the straw a little bit more to the left or to the right. This method improves your peripheral vision and can be generalized to fit everyday situations. For example, when you are shopping in a busy mall or walking on a busy road, your improved peripheral vision can make you more aware of dangerous situations (somebody lurking around and eyeing your handbag, somebody following you, a vehicle overtaking you on the wrong side, etc.) and help improve your reaction time.

b) Game time: This exercise helps you hone your observation skills as well as your memory. You can either do this when you are alone or can play this with your friends. When you find yourself in a new environment or in a busy place, ask yourself a few questions and practise your observation skills. For this particular example, picture yourself in a movie theatre. Since the movie has not started yet, you have time to ask yourself the following questions. (These are just sample questions. Try and think up a few more.)

i. How many people can you see in the theatre? How many of them are over 60 years of age? How many of them are under 20?

ii. How many men have long hair? How many men are wearing noticeable jewellery? Does any particular person stand out? How many women are wearing something unique or have a unique haircut/hairstyle? Any interesting tattoos?

iii. How many people look bored, happy, excited, angry, sad, grumpy, annoyed, etc.?

iv. How many people are wearing red? How many people have their hair in ponytails? How many people have started eating their snacks already? How many people are with their significant others but are spending more time on their phones?

v. How many exit doors can you see? How many sprinklers can you see?

Try and make up more questions to ask yourself. Have fun with this exercise. Try and observe unique characteristics of people, their body language, etc. Make this a habit when you go out. When you come back home, try and recall all the questions and your answers to them, and as you do this, try and visualize or 'see' the scene in your mind. If you play this exercise with your friends, you can see if there is any discrepancy between your recall and theirs.

Sound: By relying on sight alone for information, we miss out on our other senses. Sometimes, we listen to blaring music on our headphones and completely fail to hear interesting things happening around us. Sometimes, while we're on social media, we may watch dozens of videos on various topics, but how many of those videos would we be able to recall once we exit the app? Here are two exercises to help you be more aware of the sounds around you.

a) Blindfolded navigation: As the name suggests, you are required to either keep your eyes shut or blindfold yourself for this exercise. Try this exercise at home or outside in a safe environment. Once you are blindfolded, stop and listen to all the sounds around you. What do you hear? How loud is it? Do you hear softer, more subtle sounds? How many of these sounds were already there but just not in your awareness? Now, using these sounds, try navigating your way around your house for the next twenty minutes or so. Now that your eyes are blindfolded and you are not distracted by the sights around you, is there anything that you are hearing for the first time? Once you are more comfortable with this exercise, try this outside in a park (make sure it is a safe environment, away from traffic and other dangers). Hear the rustle of leaves on the trees, the sounds of animals and birds, traffic sounds (can you differentiate between vehicles just by their sounds?), etc. Try to rely on the sounds to guide you.

b) Audio attention: When you are at a restaurant or any other public place, try and see if you can pick up conversations between people sitting a few tables away from you. This doesn't mean that you should eavesdrop on their conversation—simply see if you can hear them. This will require you to expand your auditory awareness to skip the tables next to you and pinpoint voices and conversations of people who are further away.

Touch: Here are two exercises to hone your kinaesthetic powers (sense of touch).

a) Kitchen sense: In this exercise, you need to blindfold yourself and enter the kitchen. Try getting out all the ingredients, vessels and utensils that you need to make a cup of coffee, simply by touch. Without checking, can you picture where all the ingredients for the coffee are on your kitchen shelves? Where are your coffee mugs? Where is the water, sugar, milk and coffee powder? What vessel would you require to heat water? Where is the spoon that you will need to stir sugar? Keep all these things ready.
   Note: This exercise does not require you to actually make the coffee blindfolded—just to keep the ingredients ready. Try this exercise with other things as well.

b) Bath time: Before your bath, try picking out your clothes by touch alone. Try performing your entire bathroom routine with your eyes closed. Find your toothpaste and toothbrush, and brush your teeth. Locate the taps, bucket, mug, soap, shampoo, etc. just by touch and take a bath without opening your eyes. You will begin to notice various textures of common things around you, including your own body, that you wouldn't usually notice when you are 'looking'. This may sound a bit absurd and unnecessarily difficult, but it will help in honing your sense of touch and teach you to be more aware of textures and the placement of objects within your bathroom.

Smell: How many of us actually pay attention to our sense of smell? Humans have the ability to detect and differentiate one trillion different varieties of scents! Unlike our other senses that have to undergo a number of processes for the information to reach the brain, our sense of smell directly connects to the brain and is therefore deeply connected to our emotions and memories. This is why a familiar fragrance can immediately transport you back in time. Here are two exercises to hone your sense of smell.

a) Supermarket adventures: The next time you are in a supermarket, stand in an aisle, close your eyes and try to identify various products on the shelves just by their smell. If you know the supermarket well enough and it is not crowded, try and walk down the aisles with your eyes closed and guess the products on the shelves by smell alone.

b) Food court: The next time you are in a food court, sit at your table and close your eyes. Expand your awareness to the tables surrounding you and the various food counters around you. Going by your sense of smell alone, try and figure out what the people at the tables around you are eating, and going from left to right, try and figure out the kind of restaurants at the food court.

Taste: During mealtimes, all our senses are activated—the sight of scrumptious food, its tantalizing aroma, texture and, of course, taste. Unfortunately, most of us miss out on this delectable experience because we are distracted by our cell phones or the television. Some people even read while eating! You can make mealtimes a feast for your senses by keeping away all gadgets while eating and by following the two exercises mentioned next.

a) Eat in silence: Of course, you don't have to do this all the time, especially when you are eating with family or friends. However, it does pay to have at least one meal a week in silence. This will help you focus better on your food and enjoy it more. In the absence of verbal communication and visual stimulus in the form of smartphones, television and books, your other senses will be heightened and you will be surprised at how different your normal food tastes and feels. If possible, close your eyes when you eat. This will enhance the experience even more.

b) Potluck time: Have one day in a month when each family member or friend brings whatever they want to the table. Don't plan in advance. Put all the food together and eat it as one meal. Imagine the strange combinations this can bring about! Imagine dipping your French fries in coconut chutney or eating a roti with popcorn! An unplanned meal such as this is not only fun but also challenges your taste buds (and perhaps your aesthetic sense!) in extraordinary and novel ways, making your mealtime a much richer sensory experience.

Exercise 2: Active Observation**

Now that you have trained your five senses, use them in the following exercises to actively observe and recall images, words and symbols.

1. Object recall: Look at the following images for not more than 60 seconds and then cover them up. Then, either draw them or write down their names in the correct positions in the empty box provided.

Now, without checking back, answer the following questions:

a) What was the angel holding? How many stars were around the angel?
b) What was the design on the cup?
c) What was written on the key?
d) Which direction was the seahorse facing?
e) Are any two pictures related to each other? If so, which ones?

2. Word recall: This exercise is similar to the previous exercise but instead of pictures, you need to remember the following words that are related to parts of flowers and leaves. Take 60 seconds to look at the words and then cover them up and answer the questions below.

Petiole	Stamen	Petal	Lateral vein
Filament	Stipules	Stigma	Pistil
Style	Ovary	Sepal	Receptacle
Anther	Pollen	Bract	Ovules

a. The word 'pollen' was located in:
   i) The first line
   ii) The second line
   iii) The third line
   iv) The fourth line
b. The word 'stigma' was located in:
   i) The first column
   ii) The second column
   iii) The third column
   iv) The fourth column
c. How many words start with the letter 'P'?
   i) Two words

        ii)   Three words

        iii) Four words

        iv) Five words

  d.   How many words end with the letter 'L'?

        i)   Two words

        ii)   Three words

        iii) Four words

        iv) Five words

  e.   What were the words on the four corners?

        i)   Stipules, stigma, ovary, ovules

        ii)   Petiole, lateral vein, ovules, anther

        iii) Ovules, petal, sepal, bract

        iv) Petiole, stigma, pollen, stamen

3.   Look at the image of the butterfly for not more than 30 seconds, then close this book and draw it on a piece of paper.

Exercise 3: Observation Games**

The following are some observation games that you can play with your friends and family.

1.   **Kim's game:** This game was first described in Rudyard Kipling's famous novel *Kim* and helps increase one's ability to notice and remember details. Place about 20 to 30 random items on a tray and cover up the tray with a large newspaper. When all your friends have gathered around the tray, remove

the newspaper and give them 40 seconds to observe all the items. Cover up the tray again and ask them to write down all the items that they had seen. The person who has observed the most items and has written them all down wins.

2. **Eyewitness:** This is a game of observation where you and your friends can pick a random person in the public to observe. Observe this person for about 30 seconds and then turn away and describe him or her. See how many unique details each of you have observed!

3. **What's that noise?:** Keep your cell phone or an audio recorder with you at all times and record any strange sounds that you hear. You can ask your friends to do the same. At the end of one month, get together and play all the sounds that you have recorded and ask your friends to guess what they are. While this is a fun game, it trains your auditory powers and hones your powers of auditory discrimination. In other words, this game helps you pay better attention to the world around you and helps you distinguish between various sounds.

4. **Blindfold party:** Have you ever played 'Blind Man's Bluff' or 'Pin the Tail on the Donkey' at a party? While you may think that these are games that only children play, they can be great fun for adults as well. When you are with your friends, blindfold one person and ask them to find you. You can make various sounds around the room to give them clues as to where you are. This game hones your powers of sound as well as touch.

5. **Nose knows best:** In this game, you can fill up paper cups with various fragrant materials, such as coffee beans, lemons, spices (cardamom, cloves, cinnamon), etc., and pass them around to your friends, asking them to guess what it is. You can either blindfold them or ask them to close their eyes during this game.

Exercise 4: Observation Test***

This exercise has three questions that test your existing observation skills and two questions that train them. Take about five minutes per question.

1. **List objects:** Sit in a room you are comfortable in, perhaps the living room or the bedroom. Now close your eyes and try and list every object in the room. You can either say them out loud or write them down. To be more systematic, start listing out objects from your immediate left and pan right. Once you are done, open your eyes and see how many objects you have missed.

2. **Draw:** Using a paper and pencil, draw something that you see every day. It could be your car, the outside of your house, office or school, your handbag, your furniture, etc. Don't look at the object while you draw—you should be drawing it from memory. It does not matter if your drawing is a work of art or a scribble. The aim is to remember as many details as possible and represent them in any way that you like. For example, if you are drawing your car, don't forget the licence plate number or the side-view mirrors or the little stickers on the glass. If you can't draw the stickers, you can just write down 'Sticker of India Motors on top left of back glass' and draw a squiggle to represent the sticker. Try to put in as much detail as possible.

3. Without checking, try and recall the following:
    a) The brand of your refrigerator.
    b) The brand of your television.
    c) Is your clock at home a digital clock? If it is an analogue clock, are the numbers written in Roman numerals (I, II, III, IV, etc.) or in Arabic numerals (1, 2, 3, 4, etc.)?
    d) What is the picture on the home screen of your cell phone?

e) What is the brand of the ceiling fan in your bedroom?

f) What is the colour of your toothbrush?

g) How much money do you have inside your wallet right now? Do you know the denomination of all the currency notes and coins in your wallet?

h) What is the brand of clothing that you are currently wearing?

i) What is your full licence plate number (or your parents' or friend's)?

j) What is the cover design on the book that you are currently reading?

4. Imagine that there is a blind man visiting you at home. How would you describe your home to him?

5. Draw a detailed map of a route that you take every day. It can be a map from your home to your office or to your school. This map does not need to be a work of art—just simple line drawings will do. If you feel that you cannot draw, simply label the map. As mentioned before, the map needs to be as detailed as possible. This includes adding shops with their names, roadside trees and eateries, traffic lights, etc. The next time you take this route, look around and observe the things that you may have missed.

Exercise 5: Sherlock's Deductions*****

The fictional detective Sherlock Holmes is famous for his observation skills and the deductions he makes from his observations. Here's a short reference from *A Study in Scarlet* by Sir Arthur Conan Doyle to illustrate this.

Sherlock Holmes and Dr John Watson notice a man walking down the street looking at addresses and carrying a large envelope. Holmes immediately identifies the stranger as a retired marine sergeant. Watson is startled at Holmes' observational powers. 'How in the world did you deduce that?' he asks. The detective then offers this explanation:

'It was easier to know it than to explain why I know it. If you were asked to prove that two and two made four, you might find some difficulty, and yet you are quite sure of the fact. Even across the street I could see a great, blue anchor tattooed on the back of the fellow's hand. That smacked of the sea. He had a military carriage, however, and regulation side-whiskers. There we have the marine. He was a man with some amount of self-importance and a certain air of command. You must have observed the way in which he held his head and swung his cane. A steady, respectable, middle-aged man, too, on the face of him—all facts which led me to believe that he had been a sergeant.'

'Wonderful!' Dr Watson exclaims.

'Commonplace,' Holmes replies.

Do you think you can train yourself to observe people and make accurate deductions like Sherlock Holmes? Here are two exercises for you to try.

1. **Passive observation:** This involves merely watching and observing but not interacting with the person you are observing. Go to a public place—perhaps a train station, an airport, a movie theatre, a park, a coffee shop or a shopping mall—and observe people. You can spend as much time as you like doing this exercise but spend a minimum of fifteen minutes. Choose a place that you think will be fun and interesting. It should be the kind of place where you can sit and take down notes without bothering anybody else.

    Write as much as you can about the setting. The description should be a 'who, what, when and where' of the situation. The 'why' part is where your deductions will come in. This is simply your interpretation of events and behaviour of the people you are observing. Do you see any patterns? Do you see any unique behaviour? Is the person behaving differently or being treated differently? Notice the clothing, tattoos, jewellery and other accessories, mannerisms and behaviour of the people you are watching. Based on all this information, try and deduce their occupations. Do you think they have pets? Do you think they are married? Do you think they are parents or grandparents? Where do you think they are from? Keep all these questions in mind while observing.

2. **Active observation:** This is also called participant observation, since it involves interacting with the people you are observing. Once you complete the previous exercise and if you feel safe or comfortable enough, approach the person that you have been observing and try striking up a conversation with him or her. During this conversation, test out some of your theories. For example, if you think that the person looks like a pet owner, talk about pets and see if your theory is correct. If you feel that the person could be a lawyer, ask about it. Mentally note how many of your observations are correct.

This exercise is marked as an expert-level exercise, simply because most of us are content to sit back and observe rather than put ourselves out there and participate. However, you will need to move out of your comfort zone in order to begin a conversation with a complete stranger. You can always say that you are doing some research and get their permission to ask a few questions. Also, you will need to carry out your observations clandestinely. If the person you are observing realizes that he or she is being observed, things might get messy for you. Don't stalk them, either physically or through social media. Once they move away from where you are sitting, let them go.

With enough practice in all the exercises in this chapter, you will find that your five senses have been heightened, your power of observation has increased, and so has your self-confidence, memory and imagination. Soon, you will be able to say (like Sherlock Holmes), 'I have trained myself to notice what I see.'

WHAT MORE CAN YOU DO?

Active Observation

- Make active use of all five senses every day to train them. Follow the exercises in this chapter and apply them to real-world situations.
- Meditate or practise yoga every day. Practise deep breathing and mindfulness.
- Minimize distractions.
- Practise tunnel vision. This means directing all your focus and concentration on just one object to such an extent that everything else around it becomes dark while the object in question becomes clearer.
- Train your mind to pay attention to what's important at a particular moment. For example, if you're at a lecture, train your mind to pay attention to what is being said rather than what the professor is wearing, his tone of voice, the slide presentations, etc.
- Playing simple games such as 'I Spy' and 'Simon Says' either with your friends or with children can help you focus on things that are not usually observed.

- Other games include memory games, Snap!, Set, find-the-difference puzzles in newspapers, hidden objects games, etc.
- Some applications that can be downloaded on mobile phones to train your observation skills include Elevate, Memory Games, Skillz, Observation Puzzles, Lumosity, Memory Detective and more.
- Whenever you watch a movie, don't just focus on the characters in the forefront. Look at the background, pay attention to the music score, notice the jewellery, details of the clothes, gadgets, etc. that are on screen. See if you can find any jump cuts or mistakes in the editing. Does this movie have any Easter eggs?
- When watching a thriller, murder mystery or detective story, try and deduce who the killer is and why, simply by observing the clues presented to you. This holds good for novels as well.
- Challenge yourself to pay attention to new things. Watch people in crowded areas, take down notes of strange things that you've seen, talk to experts on certain subjects that fascinate you, etc.
- Take a 365-day photo challenge. Take one photograph every day of various things that interest you for an entire year. This will train your mind to look at the world in a different light.
- Take a course in reading body language or sign language.
- Keep an eye out for strange patterns in the world around you.

Chapter 9

Space Sense

Sense of place is the sixth sense, an internal compass and map made by memory and spatial perception together.
—REBECCA SOLNIT

Spatial reasoning is the ability to perceive, analyse and understand simple and complex images, patterns and shapes. It is your ability to manipulate two- and three-dimensional shapes and your capacity to spot patterns or relationships between them. It is important in everyday life, work and science, and plays a role in activities such as understanding complex metaphors, navigating your way around new localities, interpreting works of art, solving jigsaw and other puzzles, planning business strategies, manipulating information in your mind, and in careers such as engineering, architecture, construction, design and astronomy.

Although everyone can and does think spatially, some people are good at spatial reasoning while others struggle. Some people may be good at spatial reasoning only in one or two aspects of their daily lives but may be bad in other aspects. For example, they may be able to solve a Rubik's Cube easily and plan four to five moves in advance while playing chess, but may find it difficult to follow a map or plan a day-to-day itinerary before they travel.

Spatial ability involves creative and abstract reasoning combined with logical and analytical reasoning. Some spatial reasoning problems include combining shapes, manipulating matchsticks, matching two-dimensional shapes, mirror images, unfolding and folding three-dimensional cubes, etc.

Training and improving your spatial intelligence can help improve many functions of your brain, including your cognitive abilities, memory, visualization and problem-solving skills, imagination and creativity. It will also help you crack aptitude tests, IQ tests and interviews.

Exercise 1: Assembling Cubes*

How many of the following shapes can form three-dimensional cubes when they are folded?

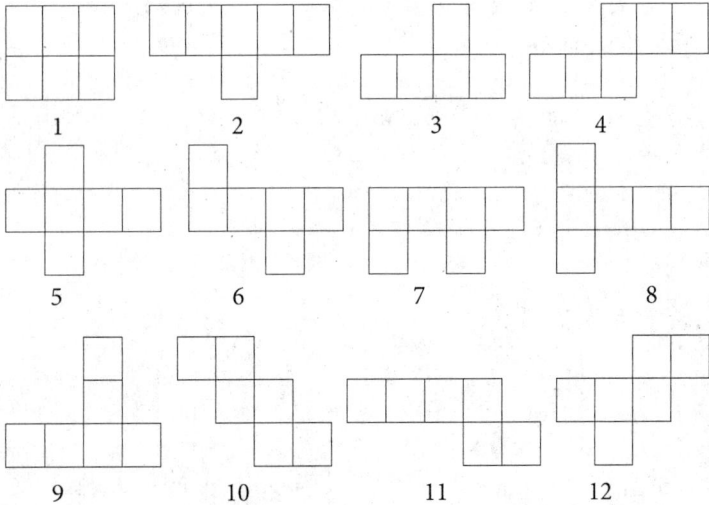

Exercise 2: Matchstick Moves**

1. Remove three matchsticks to form three squares.

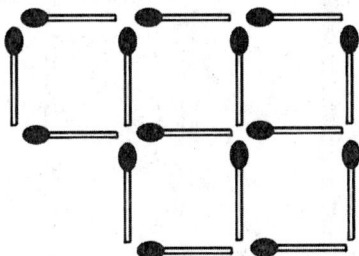

2. Remove four matchsticks to form five squares.

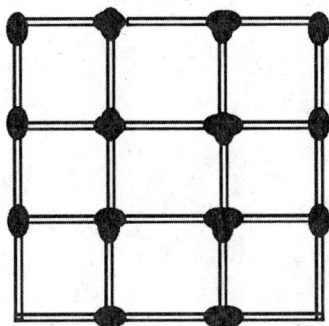

3. Move three matchsticks to form two squares.

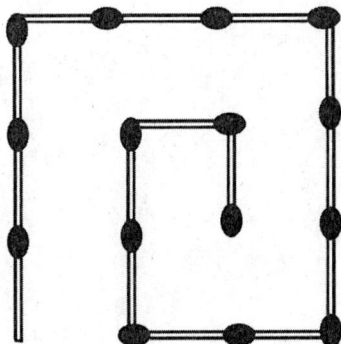

4. Here are three matchsticks. Without breaking them or adding any more, make them six.

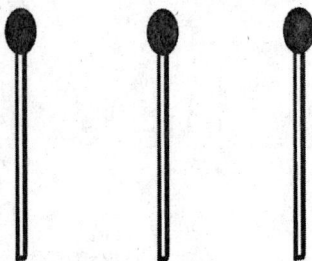

5. Move four matchsticks to form three equilateral triangles.

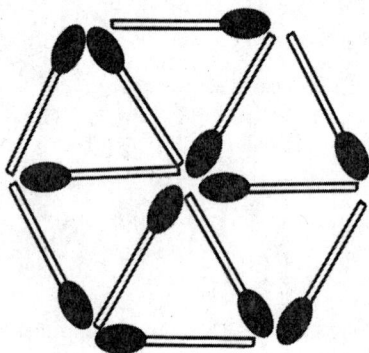

Exercise 3: Folding Cubes**

Which of the following can be folded to make the cubes shown below?

1.

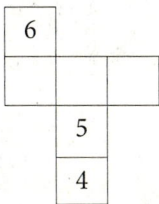
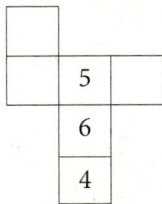
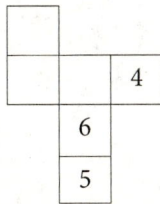
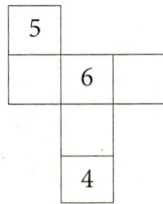

A   B   C   D

2.

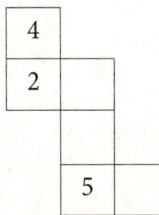
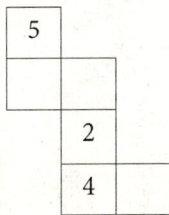
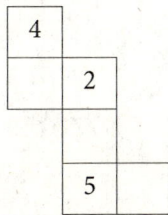
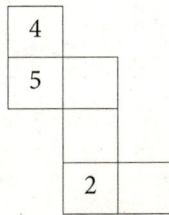

A   B   C   D

3.

    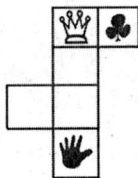

A   B   C   D   E

4.

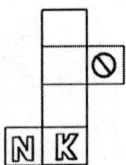  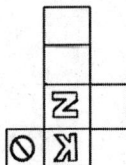 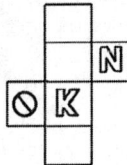 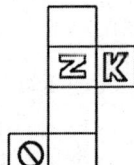

A   B   C   D   E

5.

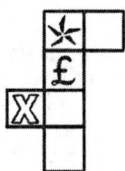 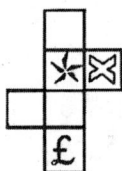 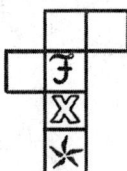  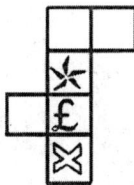

A   B   C   D   E

Exercise 4: Miscellaneous***

1. Here is a set of cogs connected by belts. If the top left cog
    is turned clockwise, in what direction will all the other cogs
    turn?

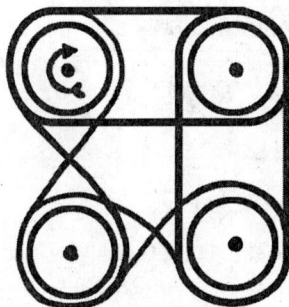

2. Which option is a replica of the image shown below?

A   B   C   D   E

3. Which shape at the bottom can be assembled to form the shape on top?

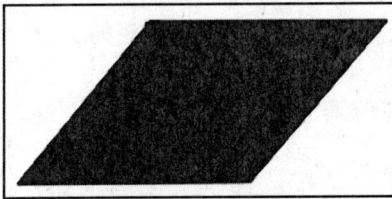

A   B   C   D

4. If you had to get the shape below by folding a square piece of paper and cutting it only once in a straight line, how would you do it?

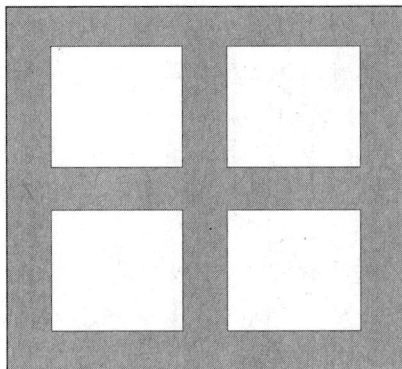

5. You have been invited to a party and have been asked to bring exactly 6 litres of juice. You have a 7-litre bottle full of juice and two empty bottles that are 5 litres and 2 litres each. Using the 7-litre, 5-litre and 2-litre bottles, how will you measure exactly 6 litres of juice to take with you?

6. Imagine that you have four round coins side by side, as shown below. Can you arrange the four coins in such a way that all coins are touching all the other coins? (All four coins have to touch every coin)

   Hint: Get four real coins and try this.

7. Look at the structure below and draw the shape from three views:
   a) Top view
   b) Front view
   c) Right view

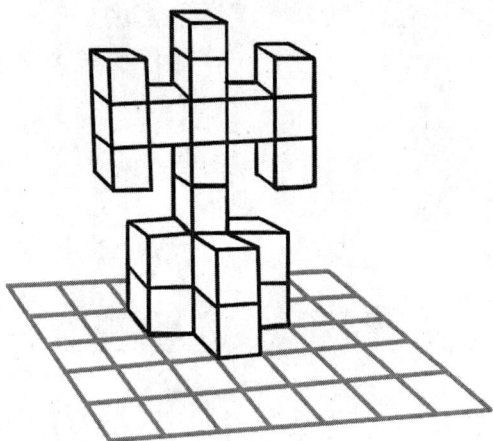

8. Which of the two images, A or B, will form the first image when folded?

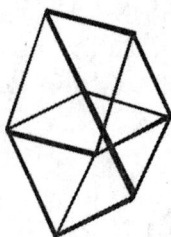

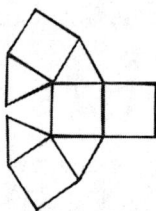

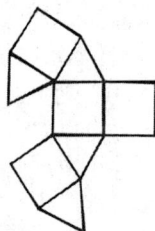

A   B

9. Each of the shapes below has an identical twin. Find the matching shapes.

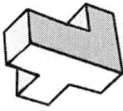
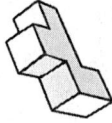
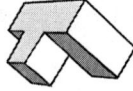
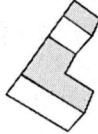

A   B   C   D

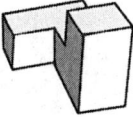
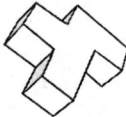

E   F

10. Which image, A, B or C, is identical to the first image?

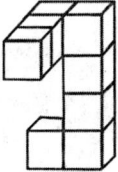
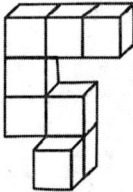
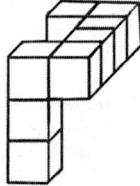
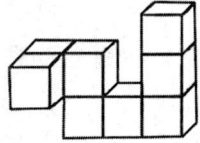

A   B   C

Exercise 5: Mirror Images****

A mirror image is an image or an object that is identical to the original but with the structure reversed in some way. It is the original image as seen in a mirror. For example, if a mirror was placed on the right-hand side of the number 7, the mirror image would be as follows:

In the following exercises, the 'mirror' will be placed either on top, bottom, right or left of the given image. Your task is to look at the original image for 60 seconds, then close the book and draw its mirror image.

1. The following is the Chinese symbol for 'angel'. Imagine that the mirror is on the right of the image, facing left.

天使

2. Draw the image below, imagining that the mirror is at the bottom, facing up.

SPATIAL

3. Draw the image below, imagining that the mirror is on the left of the image, facing right.

4. Below is the picture of a multicoloured kite. Imagine that the mirror is at the top of it, facing downwards.

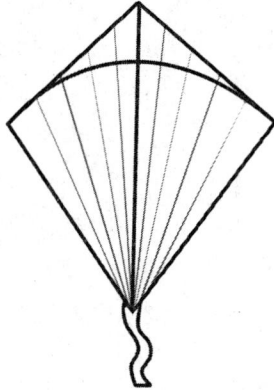

5. Draw the image below, imagining that the mirror is on its right.

WHAT MORE CAN YOU DO?

Spatial Reasoning

- Use spatial language in everyday interactions. This includes using more adjectives such as spherical, triangular, conical, large, small, short, straight, curvy, bent, under, over, behind, etc. in your speech.
- Use gestures to communicate. Learn sign language. This promotes spatial reasoning in communication.
- Make full use of your visualization skills to conjure up visual images to mentally represent an object that is not physically present. This is a powerful skill in spatial reasoning as well as problem-solving.
- Visualize a picture in your mind and then try to reconstruct it using Lego or building blocks. Try and draw it from memory.
- Play games such as darts, archery, Tetris, 1010, Jenga, Tumblin' Monkeys and other games that require good aim and spatial abilities. Strategy games such as chess help you visualize your moves and plan ahead.
- Work out tangrams, jigsaw puzzles, three-dimensional puzzles, origami, etc. Play with a Rubik's Cube. Try and figure out how to get one row of the same colour, how to manipulate certain pieces to fit in exactly where you want them to go and in which direction, etc.
- Carry a map with you and find your way through the city by navigating through it. Let this map be a paper map that you can carry with you, not a map on your mobile phone. Create a mental map of your city, office or school, supermarket, etc.
- Learn to play a musical instrument. Try playing it without looking at the instrument. For example, if you are playing the piano, try playing a piece correctly without looking at the keys.

- Learn to type on your computer keyboard, using the correct fingers for the correct keys. Practise till you can type without looking at the keyboard.
- Blindfold yourself and walk across your house, from one end to the other, without bumping into any object.
- Try following your night routine without turning on the lights.
- Fly a drone and navigate your way through busy places!
- Create a 'mind palace' to help you remember information and improve your visualization skills.
- While riding a bike or driving, make sure you are actively observing the road and other vehicles around you. This helps avoid accidents. Riding and driving by themselves are spatial activities.
- Explore your world. Exploring new roads, localities in your city, shopping malls, etc. will help you understand how space is used in construction and buildings. Get lost and try to find your way back without relying on the GPS on your phone. This has the added benefit of gaining new experiences.
- Create fun obstacle courses for your family or friends.
- Play sports such as basketball, football, lacrosse, hockey, etc., which require aim and spatial abilities.

Chapter 10

Catch Me If You Can!

Life is like a ten speed bicycle.
Most of us have gears we never use.
—CHARLES M. SCHULZ

Processing speed refers to how quickly you can process information and make decisions based on available facts. It involves one or more of the following functions: the amount of time it takes to perceive and process information and then formulate or enact a response. Perceiving information can be through any of your senses but is usually done through visual (sight) and auditory (sound) channels. Another way to define processing speed is to understand it as the time required to perform an intellectual task or the amount of work that can be completed within a certain period of time.

When your brain can't quite keep up with the amount of information coming in, it remembers the information only partially. This has negative effects on your memory, since you are not able to remember much of the information. Improving the speed of your brain helps you think better on your feet in a wide variety of situations, come up with quick solutions, react better when driving or riding, improve your reaction time in general, follow conversations better, improve your concentration and focus, improve your abilities in sports and music, etc. When the processing speed of your brain improves, your memory and problem-solving abilities also improve. This ability can be trained and improved by practising on a daily basis.

This chapter contains exercises that are similar to what you have done in previous chapters. The twist is that each exercise in this chapter is timed and you need to solve them as quickly as possible, within a time limit. Keep a stopwatch handy and write down your solving time at the bottom of each exercise.

Exercise 1: Auditory and Kinaesthetic Processing*

Time: 15 minutes

The following three problems are auditory problems, which means that they test your hearing and reaction time based on what you hear. Take no more than two minutes per problem. These problems can be solved in any one of the following ways:

a) Give this book to a friend or a relative and ask them to read out each question at a consistent pace. As soon as they finish reading one line, write it down.

b) If you prefer to do these exercises yourself, read out each line at a consistent pace, then close the book and write down what you have just read.

c) You can do these exercises as a group too. Have one person call out the words at a consistent pace while the rest of you write them down as soon as one line has been called out. See who writes all the words correctly in the least amount of time.

1. There are ten lists of one-syllable words below. The first list has just four words while the last list has fourteen words. As soon as the first list is called out, write down all the words. Follow the same step for all lists.

One, day, you, love

Life, ring, wolf, fish, five

King, ice, board, month, end, death

Time, bee, have, green, three, tree, sing

Ant, eye, star, ten, mouth, soul, rich, laugh

Dog, foot, film, lion, red, dream, key, age, rain

Ball, fire, six, wood, care, sun, cake, faith, work, self

Son, net, mole, golf, nine, cup, smile, down, land, blue, house

Ink, watch, come, high, hard, bed, rock, teen, south, rose, wish, long

Girl, hand, blood, wife, hair, room, late, big, cough, mine, fall, bell, dark

Leaf, war, list, night, goat, sin, box, two, pen, bow, fun, owl, pig, boo

Your time: _____

2. Follow the same steps as above, but this time, with numbers.

8 7 2 8

1 9 2 8 3

0 1 8 3 9 2

1 0 2 9 3 8 4

1 9 2 8 3 7 5 0

9 8 2 7 3 6 4 4 0

5 3 7 6 3 9 3 7 4 2

0 1 9 2 8 3 0 7 8 2 1

1 9 2 8 3 7 4 6 5 9 3 1

0 9 2 7 1 8 2 6 8 1 5 4 6

2 9 8 1 6 2 8 4 9 0 0 9 7 5

Your time: _____

3. The following are very simple math problems. All you have to do is tick true or false on the right. If someone is calling these out, simply mark a ✓ or X on your paper. Some questions

might be marked with an 'opp' sign, which means you need to write down the opposite of the correct answer. For example, if the question is 2 + 2 = 4 (opp), the correct answer is 'False', since the solution is true but you need to write down the opposite of it. Do all calculations and write down all the answers as quickly as possible. Try and complete this entire problem within 30 seconds.

True (✓) or False (X)

a) 100 – 25 = 75

b) 2, 4, 6, 8, 10, 13

c) 7, 14, 21, 28, 35, 42

d) G for Garden   (opp)

e) = sandal

f) 5 × 6 = 40

g) 90 + 5 = 95   (opp)

h) = square

i) 100 × 3 = 300   (opp)

j) 20, 17, 14, 11, 9   (opp)

k) 20 – 12 = 8

l) = lion

m) 12 × 2 = 26   (opp)

n) 45 ÷ 5 = 9   (opp)

o) = boat

p) 5, 10, 15, 20, 25, 35 _____

q) 9 + 8 = 17   (opp)   _____

r) 18 – 7 = 11   _____

s) = basketball   (opp)

_____

t) 18 + 11 = 39   _____

Your time: _____ Your score: _____

20–30 seconds: Excellent processing speed

31–40 seconds: Great processing speed

41– 50 seconds: Good processing speed

51–60 seconds: Average processing speed. Needs improvement.

One minute and above: Poor processing speed. Needs improvement.

The following two problems are kinaesthetic problems, which means that they test your reaction time based on your sense of touch.

4. Sit in front of your computer and open a Word document or any other writing software. Now type out the following introductory paragraph from Charles Dickens' *A Tale of Two Cities* as quickly as you can. Time yourself. Repeat this exercise five times and time yourself each time to check if your typing speed has improved. Fill in your time at the bottom. This exercise improves your hand-eye coordination, fine motor movements and, of course, your processing speed.

It was the best of times, it was the worst of times, it was the age of wisdom, it was the age of foolishness, it was the epoch of belief, it was the epoch of incredulity, it was the season of Light, it was the season of Darkness, it was the spring of hope, it was the winter of despair, we had everything before us, we had nothing before us, we were all going direct to Heaven, we were all going direct the other way—in short, the period was so far like the present period, that some of its noisiest authorities insisted on its being received, for good or for evil, in the superlative degree of comparison only.

Your time 1: _____

Your time 2: _____

Your time 3: _____

Your time 4: _____

Your time 5: _____

5. This is an exercise on speed-reading. Rest your index finger just below a line on a book and start moving it from left to right. Follow your finger with your eyes until your eyes are able to move without pausing at the end of each word. Slowly increase the speed of your finger until the words become a blur. Don't worry too much about comprehension of the material at this point. Once you have found the upper limit, reduce the speed of your finger to a speed that is more comfortable for you. Chances are that this new comfortable speed is still much faster than your original reading speed. This exercise speeds up your reading as well as your comprehension of the passage that you are reading simply by following your index finger!

Now using this method, read the following sentences aloud as quickly as you can. You need to make sure you pronounce each word correctly. If you falter, stammer or mispronounce a word, you will need to start again from the beginning. Time yourself. Do this exercise five times and write down your total time below.

1. To begin to toboggan first buy a toboggan, but don't buy too big a toboggan. Too big a toboggan is too big a toboggan to buy to begin to toboggan.
2. She saw Sharif's shoes on the sofa, but was she so sure those were Sharif's shoes she saw?
3. Which witch switched the Swiss wristwatches?
4. We surely shall see the sun shine soon.
5. Fred fed Ted bread and Ted fed Fred bread.

Your time 1: _____
Your time 2: _____
Your time 3: _____
Your time 4: _____
Your time 5: _____

Exercise 2: Word Problems**

Time: 10 minutes

1. Solve the following anagrams within 2 minutes.
   a) no more stars
   b) voices rant on
   c) press it
   d) admirer
   e) restful
   f) rotten liar
   g) nag a ram
   h) nine thumps
   i) the classroom
   j) bad credit (two words)

2. Fill in the missing two letters in both eight-letter words to form words that are opposite to each other. Solve this word puzzle in 2 minutes.

   Hint: The words need to be read only clockwise.

B	S	T
	■	
T	C	A

N	C	R
	■	
C	E	T

3. Which is the odd one out? (2 minutes)
   a) piccolo, bassoon, trombone, violin, oboe
   b) bob, mom, dad, son
   c) microwave, gas stove, computer, refrigerator
   d) tortoise, crab, frog, fish
   e) phycology (algae), ornithology (birds), biology (botany), mycology (fungi)
   f) Google, Firefox, Internet Explorer, Chrome, Safari
   g) circle, pentagon, diagonal, rhombus
   h) misdemeanour, counterfeiting, felony, pittance, heist
   i) milk, ghee, cheese, butter
   j) shawl, muffler, socks, sweater

4. Which two words below are opposite in meaning? (2 minutes)
   a) splenetic, happy, misguided, popular, domineering, feverish
   b) disproportionate, delicate, placate, exasperate, prostate, allocate
   c) apply, change, collect, advance, adhere, postpone
   d) boisterous, complacent, feasible, dissatisfied, erratic
   e) generous, dismal, magical, sagacious, foolish, ponderous
   f) amalgamate, agitate, deviate, separate, differentiate
   g) equanimity, purification, agitation, enmity, isolate

h) eschew, preview, welcome, unscrew, wholesome, metronome

i) anxious, ambitious, gregarious, aloof, concerned, purposeful

j) foolish, emancipate, decrease, enslave, notorious, patronize

5. Match each word in the left column with its correct meaning in the right column.

a)	sine qua non	feeling of foreboding
b)	carte blanche	narrow space
c)	quixotic	fleeting
d)	presentiment	of the west
e)	presumptuous	fear of foreigners
f)	interstice	essential
g)	evanescent	impractical
h)	diurnal	arrogant
i)	xenophobia	by day
j)	occidental	unlimited authority

Exercise 3: Code Breaking***

Time: 20 minutes

Try and crack the following codes in 20 minutes or less.

1. XAS AVSRKW HSR'X QEOI E VMKLX.
   Clues:
   a) There is a W in the first two words.
   b) There is an O in the first two words.
   b) There is a T in the first and third words.

2. 15, 16 14, 2, 15 10, 20 2, 15 10, 20, 13, 2, 15, 5
   Clues:
   a) There is an N in the first, second, fourth and fifth words.

b) There is an A in the second, fourth and fifth words.

3. Un petit d'un petit sa tondeur vol, un petit d'un petit a degre ta folle.

Clues:

a) The code is actually English.

b) It does not involve substituting letters.

4. G IN PO QD FE GN PQ SS UG ID FA CD FR TS UA CT VS UO QQ SD FO QZ BQ SD FE GN PQ SS UG ID FV XN PQ SR TS U

Clues:

a) The clue is in the spaces.

b) The words 'for the' are repeated twice.

5. CDJAR RUIMO ACVOC ZKENK YSDGS

Clue:

a) Think crazy grids

Exercise 4: Fair and Square

Time: 20 minutes

1. Divide the square into four parts of equal size, each of which must include one A, one B and one C.

C					
C		A			
			B	A	
		B	B	A	
	B		C	A	
			C		

2. Complete the diagram fitting the seven blocks of letters below into the highlighted squares such that each column and each row contain the letters A to J without repetition. You will need to fill in the remaining squares that are not highlighted with the missing letters.

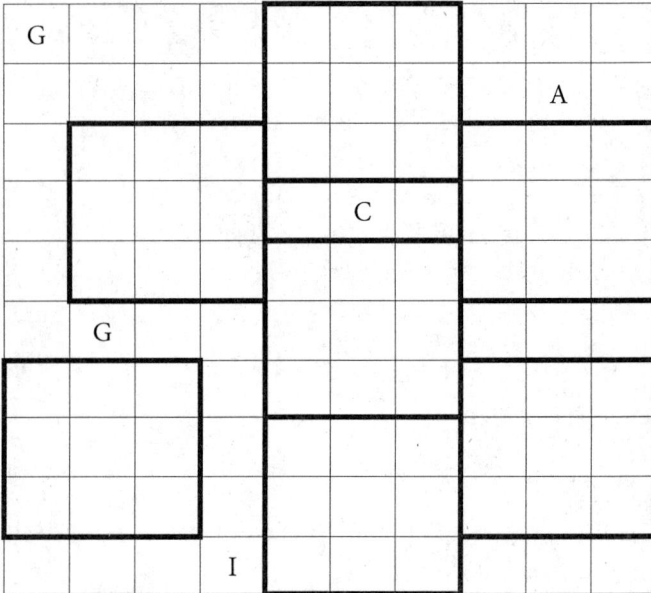

C	B	H
B	D	C
E	J	G

I	J	B
D	B	A
G	E	I

H	I	J
F	G	I
D	H	E

F	A	G
J	I	E
A	D	J

A	D	F
D	E	J
E	I	C

I	F	A
J	A	B
A	E	D

B	I	H
H	C	G
F	G	D

Exercise 5: Word Search****

Time: 20 minutes

Find and circle all the Australian states and cities in the grid below. The words can be found horizontally, vertically or diagonally, in any direction (also back to front and bottom to top). Since this is a puzzle that tests your processing speed, try to solve it as quickly as possible. Time yourself.

1. Sydney
2. Melbourne
3. Brisbane
4. Perth
5. Adelaide
6. Canberra
7. Hobart
8. Darwin
9. Gold Coast
10. Cairns
11. Newcastle
12. Townsville
13. Geelong
14. Launceston
15. Alice Springs
16. Albury
17. Toowoomba
18. Queanbeyan
19. Fremantle
20. Mackay

21. Maitland
22. Rockhampton
23. Kalgoorlie
24. Coffs (Harbour)
25. Bundaberg
26. Bathurst
27. Albany
28. Dubbo
29. Lismore
30. Wagga Wagga
31. Mount Gambier
32. Traralgon
33. Gosford
34. Mildura
35. Warrnambool
36. Tweed Heads
37. Port Macquarie
38. Hall
39. Bega
40. Henty
41. Bulli
42. Young
43. Nowra
44. Geurie
45. Hay
46. Yass

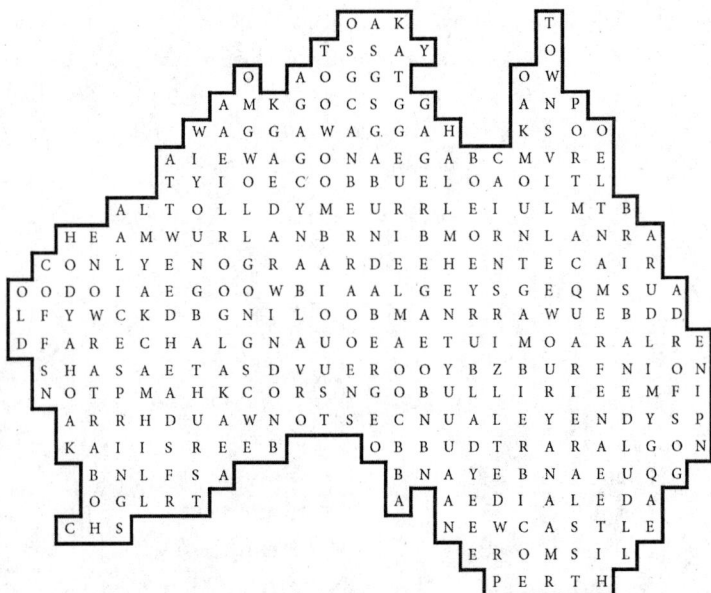

WHAT MORE CAN YOU DO?

Processing Speed

- Practise! Practise! Practise! Your processing speed will improve only by practice.
- Practise a specific skill, hobby or musical instrument. Learn a new skill and see how long it takes for you to master it.
- Look at ways to be more efficient, whether in your morning routine (to reach work or school on time) or your job, your studies, your relationship with friends and family, your leisure activities, planning vacations, etc. Work on your planning and organization skills.
- Practise yoga and mindfulness, and clear your mind of all the mental clutter that can distract you during the day.
- Work on speed tests, puzzles and exercises, and time yourself. See if you can beat your own time.
- Look at 'How to' videos or 'Do It Yourself' videos and see how long it takes for you to follow instructions and do the same thing.
- Learn to speed-read. When you study, have a mindset that you will read a lesson only once. This helps your brain focus more on the lesson than on other distractions and processes and encodes the information readily.
- Try and find other sources (Internet, mobile applications or other books) that provide you with games similar to the ones presented in this chapter, and keep working them out.
- Learn to type faster on your computer keyboard. See how many words you can type in one minute and try to increase the number.
- Play fast-paced games such as Slapjack, Snap, Set, Blitz Chess, etc.

- Play sports, take part in quizzes and other timed activities where you need to work in groups.
- Look at the cause and effect of things and see how you can anticipate what will happen next.
- Stop smoking and drinking, as cigarettes and alcohol can make you sluggish and impair brain productivity.
- Try and beat your best time in everything. You could think of a random word and see how long it takes you to find it in a dictionary or take only coins when you go shopping and see how long it takes for you to count out the exact amount required.
- All this doesn't mean that you should continuously watch the clock. Make sure that you take time out to relax as well.

Chapter 11

Memory Lane

Memory...is the diary that we all carry about with us.
—OSCAR WILDE

Working memory refers to a brain system or mental workspace that is responsible for the temporary storage and manipulation of information. For example, your mother tells you to go to the supermarket and buy eggs, milk, flour, cocoa powder and butter. A few minutes later, she tells you to buy hot chocolate instead of cocoa powder and fresh cream instead of butter. Assuming you have not written down the original list, you will need to mentally substitute one item for another. This mental substitution or manipulation makes use of your working memory.

Working memory is different from short-term memory, as short-term memory allows you to hold information temporarily and remember it in the same format, whereas working memory requires you to manipulate or change the information in some way before using it. Both short-term memory and working memory are similar in the sense that they allow you to hold information temporarily—perhaps just for a few seconds—before using it. Once this information is used, it is immediately forgotten.

There are different types of working memory. Verbal or auditory working memory makes use of your sound or phonological system. For example, any time that you listen to oral instructions, perhaps directions to your friend's house or a recipe for cake, you are making use of your verbal working memory. Another type of working memory is visual-spatial in nature, which allows you to visualize something and store it in your mind. This skill is used in mathematics and also to remember images, patterns and a particular sequence of events.

Working memory plays a very important role in cognitive abilities such as planning, problem-solving and mathematical reasoning, and plays an influential role in academic performance. Working memory improves with age. As an adult, you will be able to hold about seven unrelated pieces of information in your mind, plus or minus two. This means that even without training your mind, you can hold anywhere between five to nine pieces of information in your mind. With training, you will be able to hold much more information in your mind, even if it is just temporarily.

Exercise 1: Zodiac Signs*

Look at the zodiac signs and their symbols below for one minute, then cover them up and answer the question below.

Hint: Take note of the numbers associated with each zodiac sign.

	Zodiac Sign	**Symbol**
1.	Capricorn	Mountain Goat
2.	Aquarius	Water bearer
3.	Pisces	Fish
4.	Aries	Ram
5.	Taurus	Bull
6.	Gemini	Twins
7.	Cancer	Crab
8.	Leo	Lion
9.	Virgo	Virgin
10.	Libra	Scales

11.	Scorpio	Scorpion
12.	Sagittarius	Archer

Now cover the zodiac signs above and fill them out in the table below along with their symbols, according to their corresponding numbers.

	Zodiac Sign	**Symbol**
3.		
4.		
8.		
10.		
12.		
1.		
9.		
2.		
5.		
7.		
11.		
6.		

Exercise 2: Rows**

Look at the words below for one minute, then turn the page and answer the question.

Hint: Take note of the numbers associated with each line.

1.	Rainbow	Orange	Chocolate	Seventy	Potato
2.	Adventure	Elephant	Energy	Dangerous	Forever
3.	Jupiter	Meditate	Something	Memories	Pollution
4.	Harmony	Mystery	Library	Magical	Uniform

Now write down the words below in the order of lines indicated.

4.				
2.				
1.				
3.				

Exercise 3: Substituting Formulae**

Read the following questions once, and only once, before answering. While answering, do not refer back to the question and do not write down any of the values from the questions. The substitutions and calculations need to be done in your mind. You can, however, make a note of the answers and check them with those provided at the end of the book once you finish the entire exercise.

1. If A = 13, B = 15 and C = 20, then (cover up this line now)
    a) C + B = ?
    b) B – A = ?
    c) A + B + C = ?
2. If A = 12, B = 21, C = 7 and D = 42, then (cover up this line now)
    a) A + B + C + D = ?
    b) D – B = ?
    c) B – A = ?
3. If A = 8, B = 15, C = 19, D = 20 and E = 12, then (cover up this line now)
    a) C – E = ?
    b) A x B = ?
    c) D + E = ?
4. If A = 19, B = 20, C = 41, D = 45, E = 22 and F = 65, then (cover up this line now)

a) F – D = B (True or False?)

b) C – B = A (True or False?)

c) C – A = E (True or False?)

5. If A = 7, B = 14, C = 31, D = 2, E = 100, F = 23 and G = 17 then (cover up this line now)

a) A x B x E = ?

b) A + B + C + G = ?

c) E – F – A = ?

Exercise 4: Up, Down, Right, Left, Jump!***

1. Given below are 10 rows of numbers, beginning with four-digit numbers and increasing to thirteen-digit numbers. You can either read out the numbers yourself or ask someone to read them out for you at a measured, consistent pace and tone of voice. Your task is to listen to the entire row of numbers and then write them down in ascending order (from the smallest to the largest number). For example, if the number is 3287, you will need to write it down as 2378. If there are two numbers that are repeated, you need to write both of them down side by side. For example, if the number is 28312, you need to write it down as 12238.

3 8 4 7

2 8 3 7 5

1 9 3 8 4 7

9 1 6 3 8 4 9

2 5 2 3 7 3 8 0

9 0 2 7 1 6 5 4 9

1 9 2 8 4 0 2 7 4 1

9 1 8 2 7 3 0 4 6 5 0

5 6 4 7 3 9 2 0 1 9 3 1

0 1 9 2 8 3 7 4 6 2 5 9 1

2. Follow the same steps with the rows of numbers below, except

this time, you must write them down in descending order (from largest to smallest). For example, if the number is 374, you need to write 743.

1 8 3 7

0 1 9 2 1

1 2 0 3 9 4

5 4 7 1 0 3 9

1 9 2 8 3 7 0 1

0 1 8 2 6 3 8 3 7

1 8 2 9 3 0 5 8 0 9

1 9 2 9 3 7 0 9 7 6 8

0 9 1 8 2 7 3 7 9 8 4 0

2 0 9 8 0 2 8 7 5 3 8 9 1

3. Now follow the same steps with the following rows of numbers, except this time, write down the consecutive numbers, for each digit. For example, if the number is 276, you need to write down 387. The consecutive number for 9 is 10.

2 8 3 9

1 9 2 8 0

1 7 2 8 3 9

0 1 9 8 2 8 3

1 8 2 9 2 3 8 8

1 9 2 8 3 7 2 6 5

5 6 4 7 3 9 2 9 0 1

9 1 8 2 7 3 6 7 5 4 8

9 1 8 2 7 3 6 4 7 3 8 2

6 7 4 0 1 2 0 9 8 1 7 9 8

4. Again, follow the same steps as above, but this time, write down the number that comes immediately before the number being called out. For example, if the number is 768, write 657. The number immediately before 0 is 9.

2 8 4 9

2 9 3 8 4
0 9 4 8 4 8
4 6 2 9 0 3 4
4 0 3 9 3 8 2 7
1 0 2 9 3 8 4 6 5
1 9 2 8 3 7 0 6 8 4
1 9 2 0 3 9 4 8 5 7 9
1 0 2 9 3 8 7 4 6 8 2 1
1 9 2 8 3 7 4 6 8 3 9 1 7

5. In this exercise, follow the same steps, except you need to jump ahead by two consecutive numbers for each digit. For example, if the number is 364, write down 586. The number 8 then becomes 10 and the number 9 becomes 11.

3 4 8 4
2 9 3 8 4
9 2 7 4 0 1
9 2 8 3 7 1 7
4 6 3 8 2 9 3 5
1 7 2 8 3 7 4 6 5
2 8 3 7 0 1 6 8 3 9
1 9 2 8 3 7 9 2 7 6 9
1 8 2 9 3 8 4 9 3 0 1 9
8 5 7 2 9 4 6 2 0 5 6 2 8

Exercise 5: Word Order****

1. In the following exercise, you are given ten rows of random words. Either read out each list yourself or ask a friend or family member to read it out at a consistent pace and tone of voice. After each list has been read, write down the same words in alphabetical order (A to Z). For example, if the words are 'read, write, listen, speak', write them down as 'listen, read, speak, write'.

a) tonight, rooftop, market, turnip
b) towel, poison, tinfoil, secure, manure
c) hammer, rocket, dinner, boxer, letter, purple
d) silver, seven, heaven, puppy, angel, music, office
e) nature, twenty, husband, apple, lady, tiger, monster, yellow
f) money, broken, Sunday, body, circle, circus, lemon, baby, sister
g) China, open, monkey, secret, story, power, today, teacher, Disney, April
h) candy, winter, even, kitchen, bucket, doctor, above, many, oven, treasure, pasta
i) loving, someone, total, cookie, mango, under, zero, better, panda, happen, also, ago
j) sorry, little, spirit, ginger, ugly, cousin, couple, penny, honey, enough, colour, dragon, value

2. Follow the same instructions for the words below but arrange them in reverse alphabetical order (from Z to A).
a) mom, bike, can, dog
b) ant, yes, zoo, was, pig
c) king, jump, fish, ox, no, up
d) all, day, have, his, long, man, more
e) old, time, war, cow, cans, wolf, zebra, they
f) look, first, two, could, now, good, life, down, back
g) mean, own, great, need, three, high, keep, big, seem, hand
h) show, small, night, bring, room, side, head, sit, car, lose, law
i) line, game, bad, set, end, pay, job, case, book, five, art, such
j) stop, walk, win, both, foot, age, buy, wait, die, serve, sand, love, bolt

3. Read the following words, then cover them up and write

them down backwards. For example, if the words is 'memory', write it down as 'yromem'.

a) freezing
b) majestic
c) squiggle
d) applejack
e) maximizes
f) jaywalked
g) oxygenized
h) circumflex
i) acquirable
j) mosquitoes

WHAT MORE CAN YOU DO?

Working Memory

- Work on your visualization skills, as it may be necessary to visualize information in your mind first before you can manipulate it. Play games that involve visual memory (card-matching games, observation games, etc).

- Card games such as Crazy Eights, Uno, Go Fish, War, etc. improve working memory, as you not only have to remember specific rules but you also need to remember the cards you and other people have.

- Start active reading. This means that you interact with your reading material by using highlighters, sticky notes, underlining text or simply reading out loud. This helps you keep the information in your mind long enough to answer questions about it.

- Chunk information into smaller pieces. It is easier to

remember small groups of numbers rather than a long string of numbers. Repeat Exercise 4 of this chapter by chunking the numbers into groups of 2 or 3 and see if you fare better.

- Look for patterns and make connections. Our brains are naturally tuned to recognize and remember patterns. Once you recognize a pattern or the logic behind something, you will remember it better. This not only helps with working memory but develops long-term memory as well.
- Use checklists for tasks that have multiple steps.
- Use two or more of your senses simultaneously. Processing information in as many ways as possible aids working memory.
- Be more mindful of things happening around you. Being absent-minded is a sign of poor working memory. Practise mindfulness techniques and meditation to improve your working memory.
- Experiment with various ways of remembering information. You may remember a list better if you make it a rhyme or add music to it and sing it!
- Reduce multitasking, or do away with it altogether. Multitasking doesn't mean that you are doing two tasks at the same time. It just means that you are rapidly shifting attention from one task to another, and this can fatigue your brain. When you focus on only one task, you give your whole attention to it and this aids your working memory.
- Reduce distractions. Learn to tune out distractions or minimize them as much as possible.
- Deal with stress so that it does not interfere with your memory.
- Improve your focus and concentration skills.

Chapter 12

Conclusion

Anyone who stops learning is old,
whether twenty or eighty.
—HENRY FORD

Now that you have completed this book of brain-boosting exercises, you may find that your concentration and focus have increased, your mind has become sharper, you are able to solve problems in a more logical and analytical way, and your memory power is much stronger than before. You may find that your reaction time has improved and so have your powers of imagination, creativity and observation. What's more, your language, comprehension and ability to think laterally and out of the box have also improved. Don't stop here. Continue to train your brain by giving it more challenges to solve. Here are a few handy tips on how you can do this:

1. Scour newspapers, magazines and mobile applications for different types of puzzles, whether crosswords, sudoku (and variations such a kakuro, wordoku, windoku, picture sudoku, etc.) or other brain-teasers.
2. If you liked a particular type of puzzle in this book, look for other books or websites with similar puzzles, and continue working them out.
3. Once you become adept at solving a puzzle, try and step it up with more challenging versions of the same puzzle. Make

sure that the challenges keep getting tougher and tougher until even the toughest problem is child's play to you.

4. Keep timing yourself when you do puzzles and try to beat your previous record. This improves your processing speed.

5. You're never too old to go toy-shopping! Whenever you pass a toy shop, go in and check out the latest toys, jigsaw puzzles and gadgets. Games such as darts, carom, chess, Chinese chequers, droughts and Legos are classics and help train various aspects of your cognitive abilities.

6. Console games and video games such as Super Mario, NeuroRacer, Need for Speed, etc. can stimulate neurogenesis (growth of new neurons in the brain) and can stimulate spatial abilities, strategic planning, memory formation and fine motor movements. Play these games but limit your time to a maximum of half an hour every day.

7. Different software applications such as Lumosity, Elevate, Brain Training, Mental! and many more can be downloaded and installed on your mobile phone, and can help with brain training. Again, see that your screen time does not exceed half an hour per day.

8. Websites such as Brainzilla.com and Brilliant.org have numerous puzzles that will keep you entertained while training a particular cognitive skill. Keep your eyes peeled for other similar websites as well. Some websites even email brain games and puzzles to you on a daily basis!

9. Try and make your own brain games, brain-teasers and puzzles. Use existing formats and try and find variations for them. For example, the reverse crossword and reverse minesweeper puzzles that you solved in this book are variations of the classic crossword and minesweeper puzzles. Making up your own puzzles will also sharpen your mind.

10. Make solving puzzles a lifestyle change. Try to dedicate

at least half an hour every day to solving puzzles. This half an hour can be any time during the day, but preferably in the morning, perhaps on your commute to school or work.

On a daily basis, try solving puzzles in daily newspapers or mobile applications. Try and play some games during family time in the evening. Any card game, board game or strategy game is not only fun, but can be educational as well. On a weekly basis, try and have one game night or family night, where you and your friends and family can get together for group activities. Once a week, take at least two or three of the parameters in this book and work out problems associated with each of these parameters.

Once brain games become part of your lifestyle, your mind will be sharp and agile all your life and, what's more, your stress levels will decrease and energy and vitality will increase. With an agile brain and a sharp mind, you will truly be a formidable force of nature.

All the very best!

Answers

CHAPTER 2

Just Deduce It!

Exercise 1: Relative Relationships*

1. True
2. Mr Smith has 5 children—4 daughters and 1 son. Each daughter has the same brother.
3. Statement b) is false.
4. b) Jane's surname is Stephen.
5.

F	D	G
I	A	C
B	H	E

6. If answer 'a' is correct, then answer 'b' ('Answer A or B') will also be correct. If answer 'b' is correct, then answer 'c' ('Answer B or C') will also be correct. This leads to the conclusion that if either answer 'a' or answer 'b' is correct, there are at least two correct answers. This contradicts the statement 'there is only one correct answer'. If answer 'c' is correct, then there are no contradictions. Therefore, the solution is answer 'c'.
7. Statement 'c' is certainly correct. The only thing that can be stated for sure is that Paul is the tallest. If Bob and Jerry have different heights, one of the other statements is also correct. However, if Bob and Jerry are of the same height, none of the other two statements are correct!

8. Priya is the oldest friend and should get the extra slice of pizza. If Radha is two months older than Georgie and Priya is three months older than Georgie, then Priya is one month older than Radha. Kelly is younger than both Radha and Priya. Therefore, Priya is the oldest.

9. Kiran is in front of the house. Ronny is in the alley behind the house, Sam is on the north side and Joseph is on the south.

10. From the second statement, we know that the six people sat at the table in the following way (clockwise and starting with Priya's husband):

Priya's husband, woman, man, woman, man, Preethi

Because Priya did not sit beside her husband, the situation must be as follows:

Priya's husband, woman, man, Priya, man, Preethi

The remaining woman must be Asha, and combining this with the first statement, we arrive at the following situation:

Priya's husband, Asha, man, Priya, George, Preethi

Because of the third statement, Pradeep and Dilip can be placed in only one way, and we now know the complete order:

Priya's husband Dilip, Asha, Pradeep, Priya, George, Preethi

Conclusion: The name of Priya's husband is Dilip.

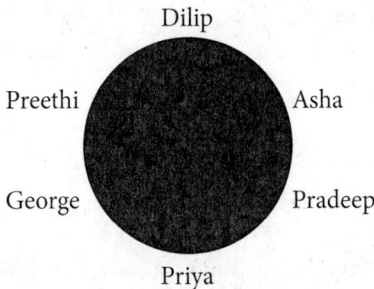

Dilip

Preethi   Asha

George   Pradeep

Priya

Exercise 2: Disconnect Four*

1.

X	X	X	O	O	O	X	O
X	O	O	X	X	X	O	X
O	X	O	O	O	X	O	X
O	X	O	X	O	O	X	O
O	O	X	O	X	X	X	O
X	X	O	X	O	X	X	X
O	X	X	X	O	X	O	X
X	O	X	O	O	O	X	O

2.

X	X	O	X	O	X	O	O
X	X	O	X	O	O	X	O
O	O	X	O	X	X	O	X
X	O	X	X	O	X	O	O
O	X	O	O	X	O	X	X
X	O	X	O	X	X	O	O
O	X	O	X	O	O	X	X
O	O	X	O	X	O	X	X

3. The exercise can be done in 15 steps as follows.
    Steps 1 and 2: Move Block 1 to Rod 2 and Block 2 to Rod
    3.

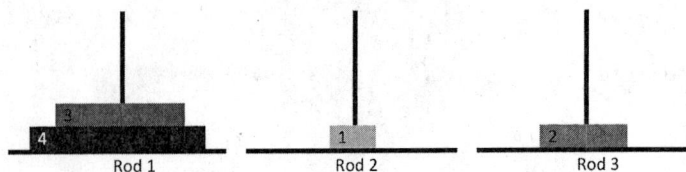

Rod 1   Rod 2   Rod 3

Steps 3 and 4: Move Block 1 to Rod 3 and Block 3 to Rod 2.

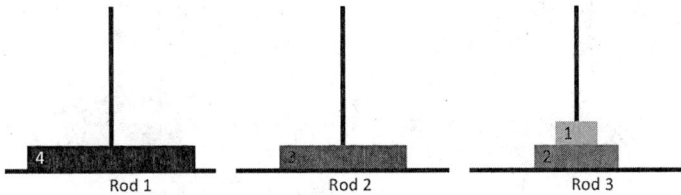

Steps 5 and 6: Move Block 1 back to Rod 1 and Block 2 back to Rod 2.

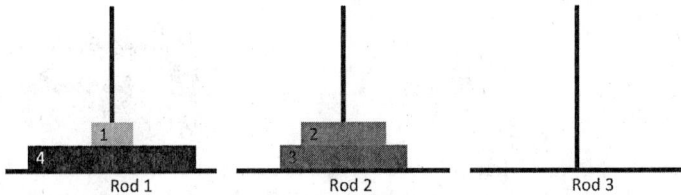

Steps 7 and 8: Move Block 1 to Rod 2 and Block 4 to Rod 3.

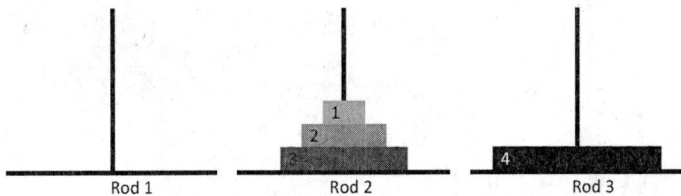

Steps 9 and 10: Move Block 1 to Rod 3 and Block 2 to Rod 1.

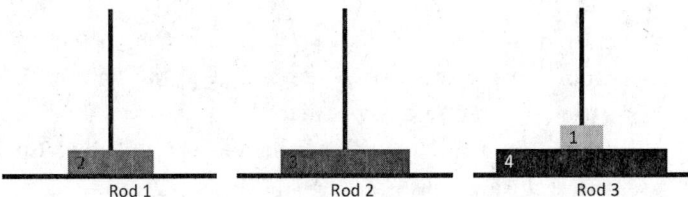

Steps 11 and 12: Move Block 1 to Rod 1 and Block 3 to Rod 3.

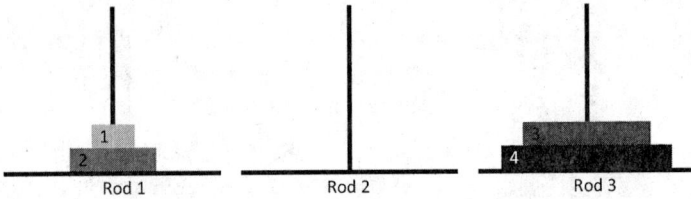

Steps 13 and 14: Move Block 1 to Rod 2 and Block 2 to Rod 3.

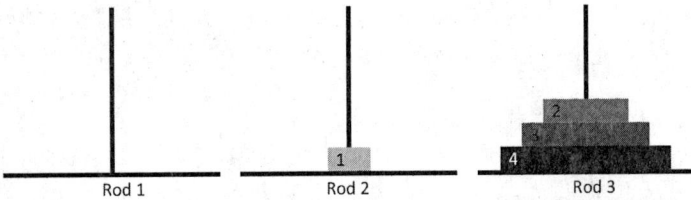

Step 15: Move Block 1 to Rod 3.

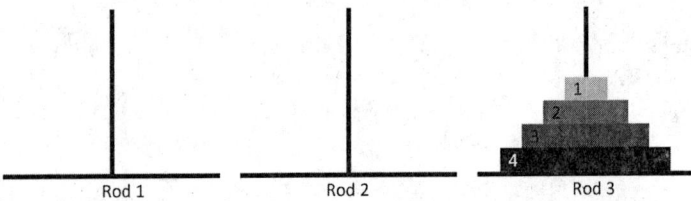

Exercise 3: Tricky Logic**

1. The man should have said 3. The password is the number of letters in the number that the doorman says. Therefore, 'twelve' is 6, 'six' is 3 and 'ten' is also 3.

2. Nineteen days. Since the lotus doubles in size every day and the whole lake is filled in 20 days, half of the lake would have been covered one day earlier.

3. One went east, gaining in the number of days while the other went west, losing days.

4. No, the answer is not 1/2 as you would normally think. The answer is actually 1/3. The following are possible combinations:

Girl – Girl

Girl – Boy

Boy – Girl

Boy – Boy

Since we already know that one of the children is a girl, this eliminates the Boy – Boy possibility. This leaves you with three possibilities, one of which is two girls. Therefore, the answer is 1/3.

5. The wise man tells them to switch camels.

6. The following might have been the disciple's thinking process: 'All three of us (A, B and C [me]) see everyone's hands up, which means that everyone can see at least one red dot on someone's forehead. If I (C) have a blue dot on my head, then both A and B see three hands up, one red dot (the only way they can raise their hands), and one blue dot (on my head). Therefore, A and B would both think this way: if the other guys' hands are up, and I see one blue dot and one red dot, then the guy with the red dot must raise his hand because he sees a red dot somewhere, and that can only mean that he sees it on my head, which would mean that I have a red dot on my head. But neither A nor B says anything, which means that they cannot be as sure as they would be if they saw a blue dot on my head. If they do not see a blue dot on my head, then they see a red dot. So I have a red dot on my forehead.'

7. Keep the first bulb switched on for a few minutes. The bulb should get warm. Now switch it off, switch another light on and go upstairs. One light will be on, one bulb will be cold and one bulb will be warm.

8. First, both children go across together. One of them (let's assume it's the son) comes back alone. Then one adult (let's assume it's the mother) goes over. The daughter comes back. The son and daughter go over together. The son comes back. The dad goes over and the daughter comes back. The son and daughter go over and the son comes back. The fisherman goes over and the daughter comes back. The daughter and son go over together and give the boat back to the fisherman. The boat crosses the river 13 times in total.

9. No, the answer is not first and second. The answer is 'Whole' and 'Half'. This is not a list of ordinal numbers but a list of inverse fractions of natural numbers. That is, 1, 1/2, 1/3, 1/4, etc.

10. No, it's not the letter E, it is the letter F. When you place the letter F on the line, it forms the letter E.

Exercise 4: What Comes Next?**

1. D is the answer. Blocks 1 and 2 repeat in blocks 5 and 6.

2. C is the answer. The black square moves diagonally from the bottom right corner to the top left corner and repeats from the bottom left corner to the top right corner. The grey square moves three places to the left in every block.

3. B is the answer. The heart and the circle move in a clockwise direction, alternating between outside and inside while the square moves one step anticlockwise and back to its original position, alternating between inside and outside.

4. D is the answer. All inside pictures move in a clockwise direction, jumping two corners. The pattern continues from Block 4 onwards but in solid shapes.

5. A is the answer. The small black dot alternates between moving one square forward and two squares back. The small white dot alternates between one square back and two squares forward.

The large black circle alternates between three squares back and two squares forward while the large white circle alternates between moving one square forward and two squares back.

6. C is the answer. The dots in each row move one step in an anticlockwise direction while the dots in each column move one step in a clockwise direction.

7. B is the answer. Sequence: mountain, valley, road through valley, valley, mountain, road through mountain.

8. D is the answer. Block 4 is the mirror image of Block 1. Block 5 is the mirror image of Block 2 and D is the mirror image of Block 3.

9. E is the answer. The solid square moves one step in a clockwise direction. The hollow circle and solid dot move anticlockwise every three squares.

10. B is the answer. If each solid circle = 1, each heart = 2 and each small square = 3, then column 1 + column 2 = column 3. The same rule applies to rows.

Exercise 5: Analogically Speaking***

1. The symbol for Libra is scales and a ram is the symbol for Aries. Therefore, D is the correct answer.

2. A marathon is a long race and hibernation is a long period of sleep. Therefore, D is the correct answer.

3. Elated is the opposite of despondent and enlightened is the opposite of ignorant. Therefore, D is the correct answer.

4. A gym is a place where you go to exercise. In the same way, a restaurant is a place where you go to eat. Therefore, C is the correct answer.

5. Candle, lamp and torch show a progression of sources of light in the same way that hut, cottage and house show a progression of types of housing from small to big. Therefore, C is the correct answer.

6. An ant, fly and bee are all insects just like hamsters, squirrels and mice are all rodents. Since a mouse is a rodent, B is the correct answer.

7. A tadpole is a young frog and frogs are amphibians in the same way that a lamb is a young sheep and sheep are mammals. Therefore, D is the correct answer.

8. A frame covers a picture just as binding covers a book. Therefore, B is the correct answer.

9. A tyre is part of a bicycle just as a petal is part of a flower. Therefore, B is the correct answer.

10. 'Examine' and 'scrutinize' are synonyms, just like 'pulsate' and 'throb'. Therefore, A is the correct answer.

CHAPTER 3

Analyse This

Exercise 1: Elementary, My Dear Watson*

1. The car was a convertible. At the time of the murder, the hood of the car was down. Once the man was murdered, the murderer raised the hood, locking the man inside.

2. Turn the note upside down and you find that the numbers are actually words and sentences! They read, 'Bill is boss. He sells oil.'

3. If Thomas was attacked from behind, he could not have noticed the attacker's V-neck sweater, since the V-neck is at the front of the sweater.

4. The number on your forehead could either be 1 (2 + 1 = 3) or 5 (2 + 3 = 5), but if the number was one, the man with the number 3 on his forehead would immediately guess his number correctly. Since he was quiet, the answer is 5.

5. You arrest the newspaper man. You notice that only one newspaper—Monday's—was on the porch, not Tuesday's as

well. The newspaper man did not bother delivering Tuesday's newspaper because he knew that the old man was dead.

6. The numbers 11-10-3-8-12-9 correspond to each month of the year. Therefore, the number 11 stands for the eleventh month, which is November, 10 stands for October, 3 stands for March, etc. When you take the first letter of each month, you get NOMADS. Therefore, the nomads are the murderers.

7. At the time of World War I, nobody could have known that it would be the first of the two world wars and therefore it was not named 'World War I' at that time.

8. The poison was in the ice in the fruit punch. Since the fruit punch was freshly made and the man was thirsty enough to gulp it down, the ice did not have time to melt. However, subsequently, the ice melted and the people at the party drank the fruit punch slowly, so they all got poisoned.

9. Windows can get fogged only from the inside, not outside, therefore Edith could not have wiped it off from the outside. She already knew that Margaret was dead.

10. The murderer is Ross. The victim is George. Ricky is not the murderer because he is the brother of the murderer. Sam can't be the murderer since he ran a marathon, and the murderer recently had his leg amputated, and wouldn't be able to run a marathon. Kevin is not the murderer if he just met Ricky, since Ricky and the murderer grew up together. This leaves Ross and George. George did not grow up with Ricky, since he was a farmer before moving to the big city—so he cannot be the murderer. Ross is still alive (he is going to instal a new computer next week), and therefore must be the murderer. It has been determined that Ricky, Sam and Ross are all alive. Kevin must also be alive since Ross plans to instal Kevin's computer next week. This means that George is dead and was murdered by Ross.

Exercise 2: Shorthand**

1. 26 Letters of the Alphabet
2. 7 Wonders of the World
3. 12 Signs of the Zodiac
4. 52 Cards in a Pack (Without Jokers)
5. 1,000 Years in a Millennium
6. 90 Degrees in a Right-Angle Triangle
7. 3 Blind Mice (See How They Run)
8. 29 Days in February in a Leap Year
9. 13 Loaves in a Baker's Dozen
10. 9 Lives of a Cat

Exercise 3: Decoding Riddles***

a) Why can't you keep a clock in jail?
   Because time is always running out!
b) What hired killer never goes to jail?
   An exterminator!
c) Where do mummies swim?
   In the Dead Sea!
d) How long should doctors practise medicine?
   Until they get it right!
e) What is the laziest part of a car?
   The wheels! They're always tired (tyred).
f) Why did the thief steal a deck of playing cards?
   He heard there were 13 diamonds in it!
g) When is a gun unemployed?
   When it is fired!
h) What has four legs and flies?
   A picnic table!
i) Where does a calf eat?
   In a calf-eteria!

j) Where do cars swim?

In a carpool!

Exercise 4: Einstein's Riddle***

	House 1	House 2	House 3	House 4	House 5
Colour	Yellow	Blue	Red	Green	White
Nationality	Norwegian	Dane	Brit	German	Swede
Drink	Water	Tea	Milk	Coffee	Beer
Cigarette	Dunhill	Blends	Pall Mall	Prince	Blue Master
Pet	Cats	Horses	Birds	Fish	Dogs

Answer: The German owns the fish.

Exercise 5: Puzzle Grid****

1.

	Superheroes			Ages		
	Batman	Spiderman	Superman	6 years	8 years	10 years
Sam	✕	✓	✕	✓	✕	✕
Bob	✕	✕	✓	✕	✓	✕
John	✓	✕	✕	✕	✕	✓

Answer: John likes Batman and is 10 years old.

2.

		Quantity					Colour					Design				
		450	500	600	700	750	Green	Orange	Red	White	Yellow	Bishops	Knights	Queens	Pawns	Rooks
Days	Mon	✓							✓				✓			
	Tue					✓	✓									✓
	Wed		✓					✓				✓				
	Thurs			✓							✓			✓		
	Fri				✓					✓					✓	
Design	Bishops		✓				✓									
	Knights	✓							✓							
	Queens			✓							✓					
	Pawns				✓					✓						
	Rooks					✓	✓									
Colour	Green					✓										
	Orange		✓													
	Red	✓														
	White				✓											
	Yellow			✓												

Answer: Monday – 450 red knights
Tuesday – 750 green rooks
Wednesday – 500 orange bishops
Thursday – 600 yellow queens
Friday – 700 white pawns

CHAPTER 4

Word's Worth

Exercise 1: Word Games*

1. a) Widow
   b) Shuns
   c) Medium
   d) Civic
   e) Typist
   f) Literal
   g) Noun
   h) Reindeer
   i) Notion
   j) Going

2. a) sword fish/ fish finger
   b) sweetcorn/ cornflake
   c) playboy/ boyfriend
   d) honeymoon/ moonbeam
   e) somebody/ body armour
   f) catwalk/ walk out
   g) birdseed/ seedless
   h) freehand/ handcuffed
   i) sirloin/ loincloth
   j) oversleep/ sleepless

3. a) Alabama
   b) Colorado
   c) Delaware
   d) Illinois
   e) Idaho
   f) Maine
   g) Nevada

h) Ohio
i) Oregon
j) Texas

4. a) JESSICA JONES
    b) SPIDERMAN
    c) WOLVERINE
    d) DEADPOOL
    e) IRONMAN
    f) AVENGERS
    g) LUKE CAGE
    h) BLACK PANTHER
    i) CAPTAIN AMERICA
    j) WASP

5.
a)	b)	c)	d)
LIKE	SAIL	FOOL	APE
LAKE	MAIL	POOL	APT
LATE	MAIN	POLL	OPT
MATE	RAIN	PALL	OAT
MATH	RUIN	PALE	MAT
		PAGE	MAN
		SAGE	

Exercise 2: Anagram Scramble**

1. Afghanistan
2. Seychelles
3. Bangladesh
4. Cambodia
5. Ethiopia
6. Indonesia
7. Luxembourg
8. Madagascar
9. Netherlands
10. Romania

Exercise 3: Across Words

1. BACKSTAB
   ABDUCTED
   EDUCATES
   ESPRESSO
   SOLITUDE
   DECLINED
   EDITIONS

2. a) P
   b) Pi
   c) Pie
   d) Pine
   e) Spine
   f) Snipes
   g) Pansies

3. a)

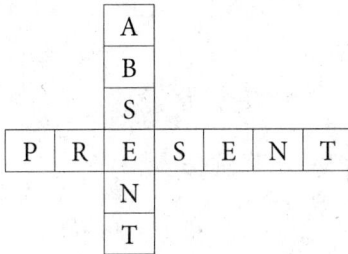

   b)

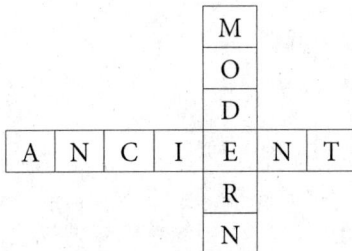

c)

D				
E				
A	L	I	V	E
D				

4. a) Buzzwords, buzzword, bourds, bourd, bords, bowrs, brods, brows, budos, burds, dorbs, drubs, zobus, bods, bord, bors, bowr, bows, brod, bros, brow, brus, budo, buds, orbs, robs, rubs, sorb, swob, urbs, zobu.

    b) Maximised, misaimed, admixes, immixed, maidism, mismade, amides, axised, deixis, imides, maimed, medias, mesiad, sammed, admix, aides, aimed, amide, amids, amies, aside, dames, damme, deism, dimes, dime, disme, dixie, ideas, imide, imids, maids, mased, maxed, meads, media, medii, midis, mimed, mixed, aide, aids, amid, axed, daes, dais, dame, dams, desi, dies, dims, disa, dixi, idea, idem, ides, imid, made, mads, maid, meads, meds, midi, mids, sade, sadi, said, sida, side.

    c) Squeezing, genies, genius, seeing, signee, eigne, genes, genie, genus, guise, negus, segni, segue, sengi, siege, singe, squeg, suing, using, zings, zing, egis, engs, euge, gees, geez, gene, gens, genu, gien, gies, gins, gnus, gues, guns, negs, sign, sing, snig, snug, sung, zigs.

5. a) Super

    b) Multi

    c) Over

Exercise 4: Box Words***

1. Zigzagged, zigzag, zagged, gazed, gaze, aged, gizz.
2. Subjectively, subjective, subject, leucite, levite, lucite, evict, evite, bluey, cite, bley, blue, cels, cite, cive, cubs, cub, ecus, etic, juve, luce, sley, slub, slue, tice, vice, vite, yule.
3. Absentmindedness, absentminded, mindednesses, mindedness, bemadden, beadinesses, beadiness, madness, beadmen, badness, dimnesses, dimness, madden, midden, badmen, beaded, mantids, enamine, santim, sadden, anti, mantid, bemas, denims, denim, bean, adenines, mabes, beams, beam, mint, mine, seam, mean, messan, masses, damn, amide, messes, admen, admit, dint, beads, base, time, times, edit, bams, sabe, absent, ament, sadness, sane, mane, manes, adenine, nine, bema, menad, basses, dedan, dimes, dime, dames, dame, meant, masse, minas, minae, mines, mesas, made, dines, dine, mead, mads, tided, tide, bead, semi, bads, amids, amid, bade, baded, names, name, nemas, nabes, nided, sabes, dabs, amen, anime, mids, minded, mind, sass, bam, banes, bane, bent, mesa, tines, tine, bani, mess, mass, bass, amin, dams, nabs, nebs, nabe, nema, emit, mina, smit, sabs, same, nims, means, assent, tineas, sade, adit, dint.

Exercise 5: Reverse Crosswords****

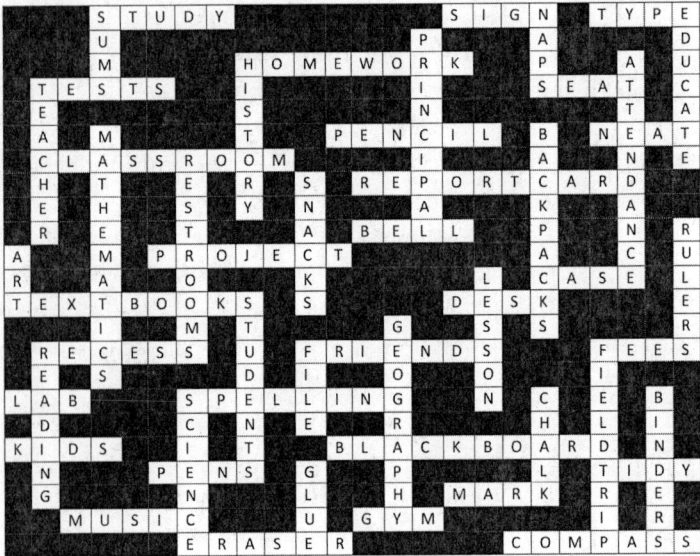

```
    S T U D Y               S I G N       T Y P E
    U                 P           A           E D
    M         H O M E W O R K     P       A   U
T E S T S     I           I       S E A T     C
E             S           N               T   A
A   M         T     P E N C I L   B       N E A T
C L A S S R O O M         I       A       N   E
H   T       E R S   R E P O R T C A R D
E   H       S Y N         A       K       A
R   E       T     A B E L L       P       N   R
A         M P R O J E C T         A       C   U
R         A O       K         L   C A S E     L
T E X T B O O K S           D E S K           E
      I     M T       G       S   S           R
  R E C E S S U   F R I E N D S       F E E S
  E     S     D I     O       O       I
L A B       S P E L L I N G   N   C E B
  D         C N E     R       H   L I
K I D S     I T     B L A C K B O A R D   N
  N       P E N S G   P       L   T I D Y
  G       N     L     H   M A R K     R E
    M U S I C   U   G Y M     I       R
          E R A S E R       C O M P A S S
```

CHAPTER 5

Loosen Up!

Since this is a chapter on creativity, there are no wrong answers, and the answers themselves can be subjective. However, **possible answers** to **some** of the questions are listed below.

Exercise 1: Divergent Thinking*

1. a) Shoelace: Can be used to tie ornaments to the Christmas tree, to tie headphones together so that they don't get knotted, as a bookmark or fashioned into a key ring, used for art and craft, or as a clothesline for doll clothes, etc.

b) Bar of soap: Can be used as air fresheners, for soap sculptures, indoor skates, helping remove tight bangles, making soap bubbles, or as a substitute for a ball when playing slippery catch, etc.

c) Empty plastic bottle: Can be used as DIY garden planters and cell phone charging trays, soap trays, decorative painted bottles and lamps, bird feeders, etc.

d) Bottle of blue nail polish: Can be used as ink, wall art, glass paintings, to draw the chakra on the Indian flag on a project, as glue to stick light objects such as string or paper together, etc.

e) Fork: Can be used to wrap wool around to aid in knitting, can be used as a tuning fork, can be used as drumsticks, or to draw lines/lanes for an ant race, to create grooves in a candle, as a comb or a weapon, or to win the slow-soup-eating contest, etc.

4. a) Type: I learnt to type on a typewriter. That girl isn't really his type. He has an A-type personality.

b) Rose: A rose is a beautiful flower. Rose fell in love with Jack in the movie *Titanic*. The entire audience rose and gave him a standing ovation.

c) Leaves: The leaves on trees during autumn are the most colourful. He leaves his shoes in the middle of the room and keeps tripping over them. He leaves the house every morning at 8 a.m.

d) Date: I would like to date that guy. My favourite fruit is a date. My favourite date of the year is 24 December, which is Christmas Eve.

e) Engaged: We are engaged to be married. The participants were engaged in the workshop.

Exercise 2: Abstract Pictures*

Possible answers:

1. Eye with eyelashes, fish with fins, sunset/sunrise, overhead view of seating arrangements around a round table, a landscaped garden with a pond at the centre, a parking lot on the outer perimeter of an amphitheatre at the centre.
2. A wave, a shark's fin, a cowlick hairstyle, a sand dune in the desert, the letter 'c' in cursive writing, somebody lying down on their side with something bulging from their pocket.
3. Flowers, windmills, large fans, art-and-craft windmills, decorative pieces, magic wands, spiderwebs, ripples in water, tiny whirlpools.
4. Snowflake, footprints of birds gathered for a meeting, arrows pointing to a treasure on a treasure map, a flowchart radiating outwards.
5. A tipi encampment, spikes on a dragon, teeth, stalagmites, jagged rocks, a school of sharks, pyramids.
6. A porcupine, a sunrise/sunset, light from a train's engine through a tunnel, arrows hitting their target at the centre, the flight path of various insects starting from one central point.
7. A monster's open mouth where you can see only the bottom row of teeth and the tongue, hills with a sea in the background, the jagged blade of a sword, snow-capped mountains, the arms of a pair of scissors.
8. Noodles arranged neatly, women with covered heads bowing to each other, pottery, rock/sand formations, seashells, a close-up of teeth.
9. Hats, shields arranged in rows (a shield wall), aerial view of mushrooms, bubbles, balloons, lollipops, targets for an archery competition.

10. Bamboo, quilling paper strips, woven straw, pattern on a wall, manufacturing rulers, straightened hair.

Exercise 4: Creative Writing***

3. Possible questions:
   a) What does a hangman read?
   b) What sign can be found in front of a dog hospital?
   c) What two things can never be eaten for breakfast?
   d) What did the lion say when he saw a group of tourists in a safari vehicle?
   e) What games do fish play?

CHAPTER 6

Figure It Out

Exercise 1: Simple Math*

1. 60 per cent is black ($9/15 \times 100$) and 40 per cent is yellow ($6/15 \times 100$)
2. Square root of 3 = 1.73. Cube root of 5 = 1.7. Therefore, the cube root of 5 is the lower number.
3. 220 (A = 1). Therefore, $10+9+8+7+6+5+4+3+2+1 = 55$. 55 × four suits = 220.
4. 33 (divisible by 3) and 143 (divisible by 11).
5. $11 \times 12 \times 13 = 1716$
6.

2	4	3	1
3	1	2	4
4	3	1	2
1	2	4	3

7. 59 pairs of socks. ($3 \times 19 = 57$ and $5 \times 11 = 55$)

8. Sophie works on 1 December (Tuesday), 3 December (Thursday), 5 December (Saturday), 7 December (Monday) and so on. Stephie works on 2 December (Wednesday), 5 December (Saturday) and 8 December (Tuesday). Therefore, the overlapping day is 5 December, which is a Saturday.

9. 33 is the answer. Multiply the first two digits and add the third digit.

    852 : 42 ($8 \times 5 + 2$)

    756 : 36 ($7 \times 5 + 6$)

    469 : 33 ($4 \times 6 + 9$)

10. The numbers 12 and 13 need to be swapped. The top sequence goes like this: -1, -2, -1, -2, -1 and so on while the bottom sequence goes like this: -2, -1, -2, -1, -2, and so on.

Exercise 2: Deadly Sequences**

1. 7238 (It's the same number, except that the numerals keep moving one place to the right.)

2. 53 (The sequence is a palindrome—the numbers read the same backwards and forwards.)

3. 0 and 50 (First digit of first number × second digit of first number = second number. First number + second number = third number and so on. Therefore, $5 \times 0 = 0$ and $50 + 0 = 50$)

4. 22 is the answer. (First digit of number × second digit of number + third digit of number. Therefore $8 \times 2 + 6 = 22$)

5. 425 is the answer. (The middle number is deducted from each number. Therefore $427 - 2 = 425$)

6. 214 and 107. (First number × 3 + 1 = second number, second number ÷ 2 = third number, third number × 3 + 1 = fourth number, fourth number ÷ 2 = fifth number etc. Therefore, $71 \times 3 + 1 = 214$ and $214 \div 2 = 107$).

7. 437 is the answer. ($7 \times 11 = 77$, $11 \times 13 = 143$, $13 \times 17 = 221$, $17 \times 19 = 323$, $19 \times 23 = 437$)
8. 168 is the answer. Subtract 4, then multiply each number by 3 to give the next number.
9. 3413 is the answer ($1^1 = 1$, $1^1 + 2^2 = 5$, $1^1 + 2^2 + 3^3 = 32$, $1^1 + 2^2 + 3^3 + 4^4 = 288$, $1^1 + 2^2 + 3^3 + 4^4 + 5^5 = 3413$).
10. 675 is the answer (First number squared – second number = third number, third number squared – fourth number = fifth number and so on. Therefore, $27^2 – 54 = 675$).

Exercise 3: Questioning Question Marks**

1. The answer is 97. The first number on the top right corner is the sum of the first two digits of the number at the top left corner. The second number on the top right corner is the sum of second and third digits of the number on the top left corner. The same rule is applied to the bottom row.
2. The answer is 2. Logic: Bottom left square x top right square = bottom right square and top left square. Therefore, $6 \times 7 = 42$ (4 and 2).
3. Starting from the first column and going down and coming back up on the right column, letters advance in twos. Therefore, the missing letters are F and T.
4. The missing number is 2. Add the top rows. Add the bottom rows. Subtract the bottom row from the top row to get the number at the centre.
5. The answer is 6. In each column, the number in the top row, divided by the number in the middle row gives you the answer in the bottom row.
6. The answer is 146. In each outer square, you square all the three numbers and add them up to get the fourth number in the inner square.

7. The answer is 20. (Left square × right square) ÷ (Top square × Bottom square) = 4 for all blocks.

8. The numbers on the right are 14, 25, 20, 31, 24, 17. The relationship between top and bottom rows is that you subtract the number 1 from every even number and add the number 1 to every odd number.

9. The answer is 2. The sum of each square is 33.

10. The answer is 329. Top row + middle row = bottom row.

Exercise 4: Placement Puzzles***

1. Shaded image

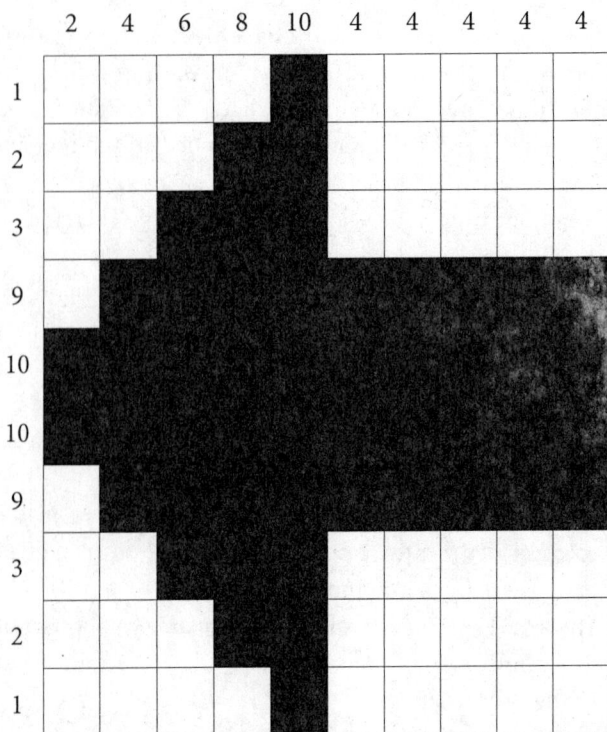

2. Pathways

61	60	2	3	4	5	9	10
64	62	59	1	6	19	8	11
35	63	58	57	20	7	18	12
36	34	56	32	22	21	17	13
38	37	33	55	31	23	16	14
39	41	42	48	54	30	24	15
40	43	47	53	49	25	29	28
44	45	46	52	51	50	26	27

3. Reverse Minesweeper

■	1		■	1			1		
2		2		2			■	2	
■	3	■	2	■	1	2	■		
	■	2		2			2		1
			1	■				■	1
					3	■		1	
		2		3	■	2			
■	4	■	■		2			2	
2	■	■	4	2			2	■	■
		2					■	4	■

4. Infinite lines

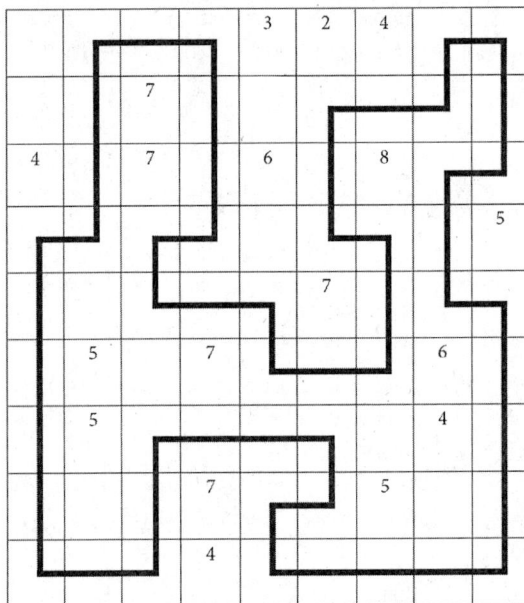

5. Carpeting

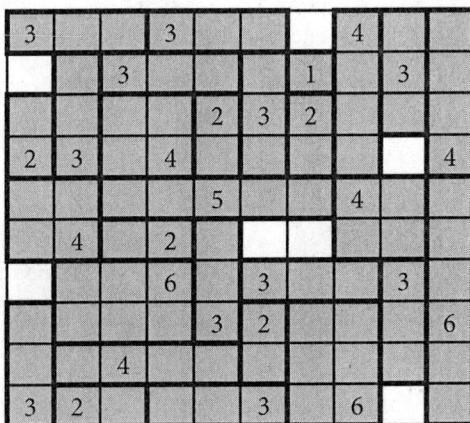

Exercise 5: Grid Puzzles****

1. Magic Square 264

96	11	89	68
88	69	91	16
61	86	18	99
19	98	66	81

2. Kakuro

3. Sudoku

CHAPTER 7

Out of the Box

Exercise 1: Brain-Teasers*

The following are possible answers to the riddles.

1. Victor the electrical engineer was the only man playing poker. All the others were women.

2. The king had given all the children fake seeds. The little girl was the only honest child who did not switch seeds!

3. There are only two barbers in the entire village. Therefore, the genial barber in the posh locality must have his hair cut and styled by the grumpy barber in the poor locality and vice versa. Since the barber in the posh locality had a better haircut, it proved that the grumpy barber in the poor locality was the better barber.

4. The man painted a very realistic looking crack on the shark tank. Since people thought that the glass would break, nobody touched it. However, since it seemed like the aquarium was unsafe, he was fired. (Alternative answer: The man stuck a 3D sticker of cracked glass on the tank.)

5. The cunning doctor's plan was to drink a weak poison before meeting the king. He would then drink the researcher's strong poison, which would neutralize the effect of his weak poison. As his own poison, he would bring water, which would have no effect on him. Once the researcher would drink the water and then his own strong poison, he would die.

   The researcher realized this and brought water as well. Therefore, the doctor drank the weak poison and then the researcher's water and then his own water and died of the weak poison. As the researcher drank the doctor's water and then his own water after that, nothing happened to him. Since both of them presented the king with water, he did not get the strongest poison known to man.

6. The man sang 'Happy Birthday to You'. This song can be sung using anybody's name.

7. The young lady was presented with a bill which belonged to the elderly woman. She had asked the waiter to collect the bill from her daughter.

8. The teacher and her class had an understanding that when they knew that the principal was on his rounds, she would question them and all of them would raise their hands to answer. Those who did not know the answer would raise their left hand while those who knew the answer would raise their right hand. She would then ask a student with his or her right hand up for the answer.

9. Jack simply wrote 'I don't know' or answered incorrectly. Jack never said that the answer had to be correct!

10. The cobbler and his wife gave nine of their children one pair of shoes each, which left the tenth pair still in the box. They gave the tenth child the tenth pair of shoes, still in the box!

Exercise 2: Riddles*

1. They were all beds. King-sized bed, queen-sized bed and two twin beds.

2. The pizza is rectangular. Cut it twice horizontally and thrice vertically to form twelve slices. Each friend then gets three slices.

3. Still 6 sextillion tons, since the concrete and stone were already part of the earth when it was weighed.

4. It was a women's team.

5. One.

6. He went to bed during the day.

7. It was a cup of coffee beans.

8. It was a coin.
9. My birthday is on 31 December and today is 1 January. Day before yesterday, I was 25 years old. I turned 26 yesterday and will turn 27 at the end of this year. Therefore, I will turn 28 next year.
10. Twelve seconds (2 January, 2 February, 2 March, and so on.)

Exercise 3: Lateral Sequencing**

1. 5 (just count the o's in each number!)
2. 2000 (it is the next number without the letter 'e' in it).
3. The letter is E for Eight (**O**ne, **T**wo, **T**hree, **F**our, **F**ive, **S**ix, **S**even, **E**ight)
4. The next letter is M for Mercury. The sequence is the names of the planets in our solar system, starting with Neptune and moving towards the sun.
5. The letter V. Each of the other letters in the series one, two, three, four and five have been substituted with numbers.
6. The answer is Ƨ. When these numbers are seen through a mirror, they spell out the word 'series'.
7. 51. The 1 keeps moving one place to the right while the 5 remains in position.
8. The clue is in the question. The central squares of the figure spell 'odd.' Therefore, the whole image reads:

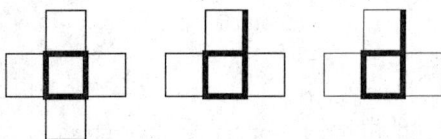

9. N. These are the letters on the bottom row of a keyboard.
10. S. These are the initials of cards in a pack of playing cards starting with Ace, King, Queen, Jack, Ten, Nine, Eight and Seven.

Exercise 4: Rebus**

1. Two connecting flights
2. Foreign aid (4 in aid)
3. That is beside the point
4. Forgive and forget (4 give and 4 get)
5. Parallel bars
6. Scrambled eggs
7. Mountain (mount 10)
8. Neon lights (knee on lights)
9. Three wise men
10. Be inspired (B in spired)

CHAPTER 8

Stop, Look and Listen!

Since this chapter is on observation, the answers are highly subjective and are therefore not provided in this book.

CHAPTER 9

Space Sense

Exercise 1: Assembling Cubes*

Shapes 4, 5, 6, 8, 10 and 12 can be folded to form cubes.

Exercise 2: Matchstick Moves**

1.

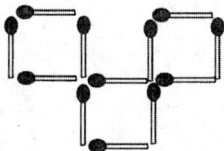

2.

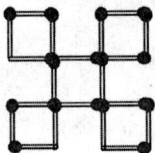

3.

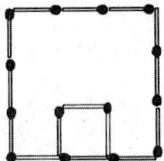

4.

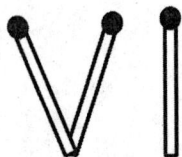

5.

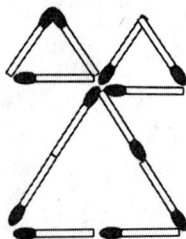

Exercise 3: Folding Cubes**

1. C
2. D
3. E
4. C
5. D

Exercise 4: Miscellaneous***

1. The bottom left cog will turn anticlockwise while all the other cogs will turn clockwise.

2. C

3. A

4.

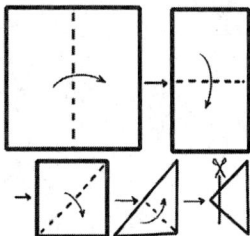

5. Let the 2-litre bottle = A, the 5-litre bottle = B and the 7-litre bottle = C.

   Step 1: Fill up B. You will now have 0-5-2 in A, B and C respectively.

   Step 2: Fill up A from B. You will now have 2-3-2 in A, B and C respectively.

   Step 3: Pour A into C. You will now have 0-3-4 in A, B and C respectively.

   Step 4: Pour B into A. You will now have 2-1-4 in A, B and C respectively.

   Step 5: Pour A into C. You will now have 0-1-6.

6. Arrange three coins touching each other at the bottom and one coin at the top like this:

7. Top view   Front view   Right view

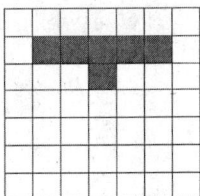  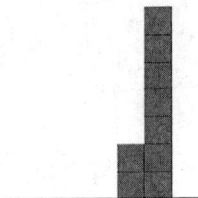

8. B
9. A and C; B and F; D and E are identical.
10. B

Exercise 5: Mirror Images**

1.

2.

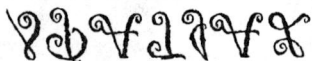

3.

4.

5.

○			✕	○
✕	○			○
	○	○	○	✕
	○	✕	○	○
				○

CHAPTER 10

Catch Me If You Can!

Exercise 1: Auditory and Kinaesthetic Processing*

3. a) ✓   k) ✓
    b) X   l) X
    c) ✓   m) ✓
    d) X   n) X
    e) X   o) ✓
    f) X   p) X
    g) X   q) X
    h) X   r) ✓
    i) X   s) ✓
    j) ✓   t) X

Exercise 2: Word Problems**

1. a) astronomers
   b) conversation, conservation
   c) priests, sprites, stripes, persist
   d) married, mardier
   e) fluster, fluters
   f) torrential
   g) anagram
   h) punishment
   i) schoolmaster
   j) debit card
2. Abstract, Concrete
3. a) Violin: A violin is a stringed instrument, while the others are wind instruments.
   b) Son: All others are palindromes (same word when read from right to left).
   c) Gas stove: All others require electricity.
   d) Fish: All others can survive on land as well as water.
   e) Biology: Botany is a branch of biology but not what it solely studies.
   f) Google: Google is a search engine, while the others are browsers.
   g) Circle: All others have straight sides.
   h) Pittance (small amount): All other words are crime-related.
   i) Milk: All others are products of milk.
   j) Socks: Everything else is worn on the upper body.
4. a) splenetic and happy
   b) placate and exasperate
   c) advance and postpone
   d) complacent and dissatisfied

e) sagacious and foolish
f) amalgamate and separate
g) equanimity and agitation
h) eschew and welcome
i) gregarious and aloof
j) emancipate and enslave

5. a) sine qua non – essential
   b) carte blanche – unlimited authority
   c) quixotic – impractical
   d) presentiment – feeling of foreboding
   e) presumptuous – arrogant
   f) interstice – narrow space
   g) evanescent – fleeting
   h) diurnal – by day
   i) xenophobia – fear of foreigners
   j) occidental – of the west

Exercise 3: Code Breaking***

1. Two wrongs don't make a right. Code: Each letter has been replaced by the fourth letter that comes after it in the alphabet. Therefore, A = D, B = E, X = B, Y = C, Z = D, and so on.

2. No man is an island. Code: Convert the numbers to their corresponding letters. Therefore, 1 = A, 2 = B, 3 = C and so on. Once this is done, each letter is replaced by the next letter of the alphabet. Therefore, A = B, B = C, C = D, and so on.

3. Humpty Dumpty sat on the wall, Humpty Dumpty had a great fall. Code: It is a phonetic code. Simply read it out loud.

4. Hope for the best but prepare for the worst. Code: Fill in each gap with the letter of the alphabet that lies between the two letters on either side. For example, for the first word 'HOPE', the 'h' lies between the 'g' and 'i', the 'o' lies between

the 'n' and 'p', the 'p' lies between the 'o' and 'q' and the 'e' lies between the 'd', and 'f'.

5. Crazy ducks jived among rocks. Code: Just put all the words one under the other in a grid and read the columns. Alternate code: The first letters of each word make up the first word, the second letters of each word make up the second word and so on.

Exercise 4: Fair and Square

1.

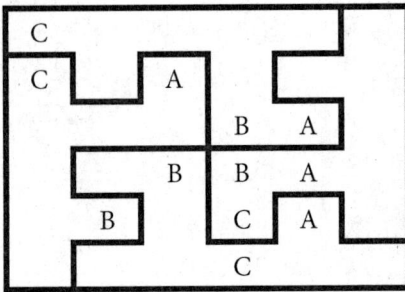

2.

G	B	E	F	H	I	J	A	D	C
J	H	B	D	F	G	I	C	A	E
C	F	A	G	D	H	E	I	J	B
H	J	I	E	G	C	F	D	B	A
F	A	D	J	C	B	H	G	E	I
I	G	H	A	B	D	C	E	F	J
A	D	F	C	E	J	G	B	I	H
D	E	J	B	I	F	A	H	C	G
E	I	C	H	J	A	B	F	G	D
B	C	G	I	A	E	D	J	H	F

Exercise 5: Word Search**

CHAPTER 11

Memory Lane

Exercise 3: Substituting Formulae**

1. a) 35
    b) 2
    c) 48
2. a) 82
    b) 21
    c) 9
3. a) 7
    b) 120
    c) 32

4. a) True
   b) False
   c) True
5. a) 9800
   b) 69
   c) 70

Exercise 4: Up, Down, Right, Left, Jump!***

1. 3 4 7 8
   2 3 5 7 8
   1 3 4 7 8 9
   1 3 4 6 8 9 9
   0 2 2 3 3 5 7 8
   0 1 2 4 5 6 7 9 9
   0 1 1 2 2 4 4 7 8 9
   0 0 1 2 3 4 5 6 7 8 9
   0 1 1 2 3 3 4 5 6 7 9 9
   0 1 1 2 2 3 4 5 6 7 8 9 9

2. 8 7 3 1
   9 2 1 1 0
   9 4 3 2 1 0
   9 7 5 4 3 1 0
   9 8 7 3 2 1 1 0
   8 8 7 6 3 3 2 1 0
   9 9 8 8 5 3 2 1 0 0
   9 9 9 8 7 7 6 3 2 1 0
   9 9 8 8 7 7 4 3 2 1 0 0
   9 9 8 8 8 7 5 3 2 2 1 0 0

3. 3 9 4 10
   2 10 3 9 1
   2 8 3 9 4 10
   1 2 10 9 3 9 4

    2 9 3 10 3 4 9 9
    2 10 3 9 4 8 3 7 6
    6 7 5 8 4 10 3 10 1 2
    10 2 9 3 8 4 7 8 6 5 9
    10 2 9 3 8 4 7 5 8 4 9 3
    7 8 5 1 2 3 1 10 9 2 8 10 9
4. 1 7 3 8
    1 8 2 7 3
    9 8 3 7 3 7
    3 5 1 8 9 2 3
    3 9 2 8 2 7 1 6
    0 9 1 8 2 7 3 5 4
    0 8 1 7 2 6 9 5 7 3
    0 8 1 9 2 8 3 7 4 6 8
    0 9 1 8 2 7 6 3 5 7 1 0
    0 8 1 7 2 6 3 5 7 2 8 0 6
5. 5 6 10 6
    4 11 5 10 6
    11 4 9 6 2 3
    11 4 10 5 9 3 9
    6 8 5 10 4 11 5 7
    3 9 4 10 5 9 6 8 7
    4 10 5 9 2 3 8 10 5 11
    3 11 4 10 5 9 11 4 9 8 11
    3 10 4 11 5 10 6 11 5 2 3 11
    10 7 9 4 11 6 8 4 2 7 8 4 10

Exercise 5: Word Order****

1. a) market, rooftop, tonight, turnip
    b) manure, poison, secure, tinfoil, towel
    c) boxer, dinner, hammer, letter, purple, rocket
    d) angel, heaven, music, office, puppy, seven, silver

e) apple, husband, lady, monster, nature, tiger, twenty, yellow

f) baby, body, broken, circle, circus, lemon, money, sister, Sunday

g) April, China, Disney, monkey, open, power, secret, story, teacher, today

h) above, bucket, candy, doctor, even, kitchen, many, oven, pasta, treasure, winter

i) ago, also, better, cookie, happen, loving, mango, panda, someone, total, under, zero

j) colour, couple, cousin, dragon, enough, ginger, honey, little, penny, sorry, spirit, ugly, value

2. a) mom, dog, can, bike

b) zoo, yes, was, pig, ant

c) up, ox, no, king, jump, fish

d) more, man, long, his, have, day, all

e) zebra, wolf, war, time, they, old, cow, cans

f) two, now, look, life, good, first, down, could, back

g) three, seem, own, need, mean, keep, high, hand, great, big

h) small, sit, side, show, room, night, lose, law, head, car, bring

i) such, set, pay, line, job, game, five, end, case, book, bad, art

j) win, walk, wait, stop, serve, sand, love, foot, die, buy, both, bolt, age

Workbook

The following section contains a workbook with a combination of questions from all the parameters discussed in this book (not necessarily in the same order). The parameters are logical reasoning, analytical thinking, verbal reasoning, creativity and imagination, numerical reasoning, lateral thinking, active observation, spatial reasoning, processing speed and working memory. This section will take approximately 1 hour to complete.

1. Which is the odd one out?
   Sow, Doe, Jenny, Cob, Ewe

2. Insert the letters below in the blank spaces to form two words that are antonyms.
   X B U F S B E O L R
   ___ L ___ ___ I ___ ___ E ___ T ___ ___ B ___ ___ N

3. Unscramble the letters K J S C T E A to form:
   a) 1 seven-letter word
   b) 2 six-letter words
   c) 3 five-letter words
   d) 4 four-letter words

4. Imagine that you are sitting on a park bench and waiting for a friend. You have forgotten to bring your mobile phone, storybook or any other source of entertainment. Your friend is more than fifteen minutes late and you are starting to get bored. Look around you and see how you can inject a touch of excitement in this otherwise boring situation. Let your

imagination run wild. Could that man over there be a spy? Could that bird be cooing out a coded message? Embellish your situation as much as you can and make it as exciting as possible.

5. Find the number that replaces the question mark.

   Hint: The top three rows are related in some way.

6	5	10
7	4	8
3	9	7
3	?	4

6. Tanya and Louisa arrived at their hotel. 'This hotel has ten storeys!' Louisa exclaimed, awestruck by the height of the building. 'Yes,' agreed Tanya. 'But can you tell me which floor is above the floor below the floor, below the floor above the floor, below the floor above the 5th? Louisa couldn't find the answer. Can you?

7. Little Billy was 4 years old and both his parents were dead. His guardian put him on a train to send him to a new home in the country. Billy could neither read nor write nor remember the address, so his guardian wrote down the address and destination on a piece of paper and tied it securely around his neck. However, despite the best efforts of the railway staff, Billy never arrived at his new home. Why?

   (**Hint:** This is a lateral-logic puzzle.)

8. Jacob and John arrive at the racecourse just in time to see the first race between five horses. Shadowfax, Firefoot, Arod, Brego and Roheryn.

Shadowfax finished in front of Firefoot but behind Arod. Brego finished in front of Roheryn but behind Firefoot. In which order did they all finish the race?

9. In my family, each girl has an equal number of brothers and sisters but each boy has twice as many sisters than brothers. How many boys and girls are there in my family?

10. Matilda and Gertrude set their watches to the same time. Unknown to them, Gertrude's watch was running 2 minutes per hour too slow and Matilda's was running 1 minute per hour too fast. Later, when they checked their watches again, they discovered that Matilda's watch was 1 hour ahead of Gertrude's. How long had it been since they originally set their watches?

11. A police detective received a baffling note from a murderer informing him of where his next murders would be committed. The note read, 'Solo pairs hasten avenge.' The detective immediately mobilized the police force in various cities. Can you decipher the note?

12. You can enhance your observation skills by practising the following steps on any random object in your house.

   a) Take any household object. It can be something as mundane as a spoon or a water bottle. Assuming you choose a spoon, study it for about 15–20 seconds to observe as many aspects of it as possible.

   b) Now close your eyes and recall as many details of the spoon as possible. Try to see it in your mind. To begin with, all you may be able to recall is the general shape of the spoon or its coloured handle. Now open your eyes and take in more detail, such as any engraving or maybe the manufacturer's name.

    c) Close your eyes once more and add your new observations to the original mental picture. Then open your eyes again to observe the spoon more detail. Keep repeating this pattern of 'open eyes–observe–close eyes–recall, until you have absorbed as many features of the spoon as possible.

    d) Now, without looking at the spoon, try to draw it, using the mental image that you have of it. The drawing does not need to be perfect—it just needs to have all the elements that you observed about the spoon in it.

    e) Try this exercise every day with a different object.

13. The following is an exercise to test your processing speed, so try and finish it as quickly as possible, preferably under 15 minutes. This exercise is twofold:

    a) Unscramble the words

    b) Fill them into the crossword grid below.

Hint: This puzzle is Halloween-themed. All jumbled words are aspects of Halloween.

Across	**DOWN**
EDHNTAU	SSIIPRT
NSBLGIO	YNDAC
EAEWNHOLL	SSOUMCET
RCSYA	DOACURNL
NOTELEKS	HOGSST
KLCAB SCTA (two words)	PPKUMNI
GIRHTF	RTTEA
PRECYE	STBA
RIDESP	EID
	CTHEWIS

14. This is a test of working memory as well as spatial memory. There are 25 rivers listed below. You need to make a mental note of their location within the grid. You don't have to learn the names of the rivers themselves. Take 60 seconds to observe the grid below, then cover it and read the instruction below.

Ganges	Mississippi River	Rhine	Zambezi	Danube
Congo River	Sutlej	Thames	Blue Nile	Euphrates
River Jordan	Beas River	Vistula	Yangtze	Tigris
Niger	Amazon River	Yukon	Ural River	Missouri River
Rio Grande	Yellow River	Tagus	Yamuna	Seine

Now, place the rivers in the correct boxes below. The list of rivers is given below.

Seine, Ganges, Danube, Rio Grande, Tigris, Yamuna, Vistula, Amazon River, Ural River, Zambezi, Congo River, Beas River, Thames, Missouri River, River Jordan, Niger, Yukon, Tagus, Euphrates, Blue Nile, Yellow River, Rhine, Mississippi River, Sutlej, Yangtze.

15. Looking at the grid in Question 14, which river is above the river which is to the left of the river that is below the river which is to the right of the river which is to the right of the river which is just above Seine?

16. Which letter comes next in this pattern?
    Hint: There are two possible answers.

    B C D G J O ?

17. What is common to the following words?
    Whine   Rhumb   Coax   Jinn

18. Complete the following sudoku puzzle in 10 minutes or less.
    Rules: Fill in the grid so that each row, column and 3×3 box contains all the numbers from 1 to 9 only once.

		5	6	9	8	3		
	9						7	
6			7		4			5
9								6
5								8
8		3				1		7
4			8	3	6			2
	5						6	
		6	5	2	1	7		

19. Write a short story beginning and ending with the following. The story can be of any length but needs to be over 300 words. The first news of activity reached me while I was eating my breakfast…………………………………
……………………I opened the door, and all noise stopped.

20. If today is three days after Tuesday, and tomorrow is five days before my birthday, what day is my birthday?

Answers

1. Cob. Cob is a male swan while all the other words are female animals.

2. FLEXIBLE, STUBBORN

3. Jackets, jacket, casket, cakes, caste, cesta, jacks, jakes, jeats, ketas, sceat, skate, stack, stake, taces, tacks, tajes, takes, teaks, aces, acts, aesc, akes, ates, cake, case, cask, cast, cate, cats, ceas, east, eats, jack, jake, jaks, jeat. Jest. Jets, kaes, kats, keas, kest, keta, kets, sack, sake, sate, scat, seat, sect, sekt, seta, skat, sket, tace, tack, taes, take, taks, task, teak, teas, tecs.

5.

6	X 5	– 10	= 20
7	X 4	– 8	= 20
3	X 9	– 7	= 20
3	X 8	– 4	= 20

6. The sixth floor

7. Little Billy was a billy goat who ate up the label tied around his neck and so nobody knew where he was supposed to go!

8. First place – Arod

    Second place – Shadowfax
    Third place – Firefoot
    Fourth place – Brego
    Fifth place – Roheryn

9. Four girls and three boys

10. 20 hours

11. Each word is an anagram of a city—Oslo, Paris, Athens and Geneva.

13.

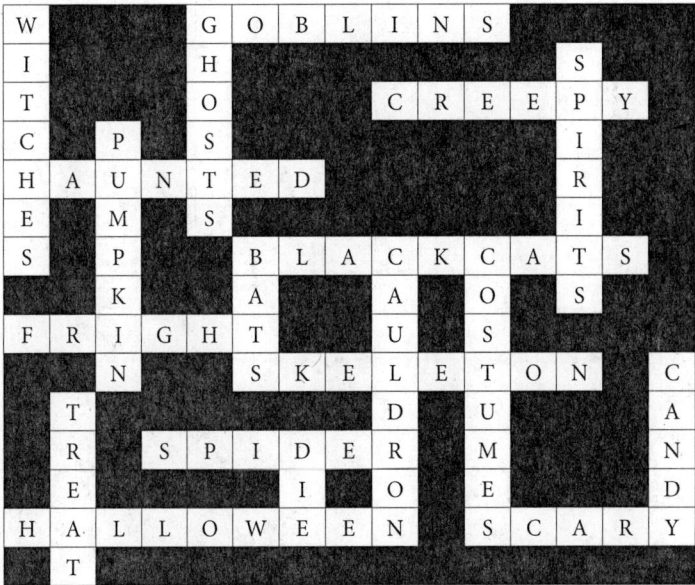

15. Blue Nile

16. P (Only curved capital letters are shown.)

    T (The letters are 1, 1, 3, 3, 5, 5, etc. apart)

17. They are all homophones (similar-sounding words) of drinks: wine, rum, cokes, gin!

18.

7	4	5	6	9	8	3	2	1
1	9	8	2	5	3	6	7	4
6	3	2	7	1	4	9	8	5
9	2	7	1	8	5	4	3	6
5	1	4	3	6	7	2	9	8
8	6	3	9	4	2	1	5	7
4	7	9	8	3	6	5	1	2
2	5	1	4	7	9	8	6	3
3	8	6	5	2	1	7	4	9

20. Thursday

Acknowledgements

Once again, a very special thank you to Yamini Chowdhury of Rupa Publications for this wonderful opportunity. A huge thank you to the multi-talented Ritabrata Joardar for his beautiful illustrations. Special thanks to my husband Rabin Stephen, my daughters Shifrah and Annika, and my parents Reginald Solomon and Shantha Solomon for their enduring love and support throughout the whole writing process.